YOU ARE NOT ALONE

You Are Not Alone

YOU ARE NOT ALONE

You Are Not Alone

How a mother's fight to save her son launched a pioneering substance addiction support group

Dorothea Bickerton

YOU ARE NOT ALONE

YOU ARE NOT ALONE

Contents

YOU ARE NOT ALONE

Introduction

Guilt and helplessness can paralyse a parent who feels powerless to prevent their child's suffering. Our mother wrote this memoir to unburden herself of those feelings. But *You Are Not Alone* reverberates far beyond one family's crisis: It is a message of hope to anyone struggling with the agonies of addiction.

Mum wrote this book in 2003, self-publishing it a few years later under the title *A Life Remembered*. We are publishing this new second edition, 20 years on, because her work is far from finished. Depressingly, the story this book tells is as commonplace today as it was back then. Today there are support services (some of which can be found in the appendix to this edition), something that did not exist in the last century. That development is, and continues to be, largely thanks to the efforts of mum and others like her: Ordinary, unremarkable people doing work that is wholly extraordinary.

Because she had suffered the awful emptiness and isolation felt by a parent whose child is seemingly beyond their help, mum was committed to helping others battling addiction. She founded and ran Family Support Group for the Relatives of Drug Users – renamed Community Drug Helpline – which would expand and flourish to become what is today: CDARS (Community Drug and Alcohol Recovery Services), one of the UK's leading support services.

Mum had grown up in the world of the theatre, and so was no prude. But the pain and chaos caused by addicts to themselves and those who love them was far beyond her experience. Her response was to empower herself. She educated herself to understand the grim truths of addiction, forging close relationships with leading figures in the health sector, including with the late Dr Hamid Ghodse, of St George's Hospital, South London. Dr Ghodse recognised in mum someone not only strong enough, but also smart enough to play a leading role in providing a type of support that was entirely absent at the time.

Supported by Dad and working mostly from our dining room, she was a whirlwind of action: feeding families who couldn't afford food and finding ways to heat their homes when they had no money for heating. She opened routes to treatment and counselling and battled authorities to bend rigid regulations and secure funding. There were no days off for her because there are no days off for alcoholism or addiction. More than once an addict turned up unannounced, distraught and desperate, to be warmly invited in, to share a meal.

Mum used to joke that they would one day build a statue in her honour in the town square. In truth, she sought no acclaim. Her rewards were mostly small, but those little victories mattered: a smile or a thank you from someone whom the rest of the world had given up on; whose dignity she had – even if, sometimes, only briefly – restored.

We hope Mum's story shines some light in the darkness for anyone trapped amid the devastation of addiction – users, their families, and those who care for them. For it is the story of a mother and her son, a testament to the abiding and enduring power of love.

Cheryl, Ian, and Michael Bickerton
January 2023

Foreword

I met Dorothea Bickerton in 1997 and had the privilege of working alongside her until her retirement in 2000 from what is now known as CDARS (Community Drug and Alcohol Recovery Services). It was my first job in the field, following my own recovery from drug addiction, and after I had spent many years studying psychology and counselling during my recovery journey. Dorothea gave me the opportunity to forge a new career, and I learnt so much from her. I wouldn't be where I am today without her. So, it was an honour when her daughter, Cheryl, asked me if I'd write this preface.

You Are Not Alone captures Dorothea's experience, not only as the mother of a drug addict, but a professional in the field of substance abuse. It shares her perspective, ideas, and approach towards drug rehabilitation. It is a philosophy that has touched the lives of so many who have struggled with drug or alcohol misuse, and which has helped and supported the families that suffer alongside them.

This is a book for those struggling with addiction, for those that have a loved one battling with this disease, and for anyone working in the field of alcohol and drug misuse. Many other books on the subject, and many clinical centres, treat the addict as a statistic rather than as an individual who is suffering deeply. By contrast, Dorothea brought a sincere and heartfelt authenticity to rehabilitation and substance abuse recovery, believing that each addict should be treated with dignity, empathy, compassion, kindness, and respect. It is an ethos that lives on in CDARS.

Dorothea was a role model for me and remains a constant reminder that we must strive to ensure that vulnerable people struggling with addiction feel heard, seen, and understood. Her compassion has made me who I am today, and I will continue to share her teachings and beliefs with the CDARS team to carry out her profound and positive work.

Franco Toma, CEO
CDARS
(Community Drug and Alcohol Recovery Services)

Note:

The support group that Dorothea Bickerton founded was originally known as *Family Support Group for the Relatives of Drug Users.*

The group became a charitable company, registered as *Family Support Drug Line*

Several name changes have taken place to reflect the expanding remit of the group over the years:

Community Drug Helpline

Community Drug Service for South London

CDARS (Community Drug and Alcohol Recovery Services)

YOU ARE NOT ALONE

This book is dedicated to Joss and the late Rosemary Ackland, in gratitude and with much love for all their support and faith in me over the years.

YOU ARE NOT ALONE

Chapter 1

Birth

I remember so vividly the events that led to your birth. On October 26, 1958, Dad and I went to the local cinema in Sutton Coldfield to see *'Ice Cold in Alex'*. You were almost a week overdue, but because we both wanted to see this film and I felt reasonably well, we braved it. I remember sitting in the darkened auditorium struggling to concentrate and feeling more and more uncomfortable. You lay still and heavy in my womb; our first child, conceived in our first year of marriage, and eagerly awaited by both sides of the family as the first grandchild. I began to have sharp pains, closely followed by a gripping backache. Tugging at Derek's sleeve, I whispered that I felt something was happening. We left the cinema in a hurry to return home and collect the bag I had packed for the nursing home where I was booked for the confinement, thankfully only a short car ride from our home in Wylde Green. Everyone thought your arrival was imminent but, like so much that would happen with you David, it proved not to be that simple. Perhaps, a premonition of what was to come, you decided to remain a little longer in this safe place rather than meet the world. And so, my labour proved long and exhausting for both of us, and it was only after four days and many complications, including a nightmare ambulance drive to Loveday Street Maternity Hospital, in Birmingham city centre, that you were finally born on Friday October 31 at 8.10pm.

You were a beautiful boy, with a rosy glow to your skin and a mop of dark, damp hair. Seven pounds and eight ounces of pure happiness. The feeling of warmth and protection that bonds a mother and child remains a force between them forever. I delighted in holding you to my breast and watching you suckle greedily. Pride and love flowed to you, establishing our bond so quietly and surely from those very first moments. Surely, I imagined, from such wonderful beginnings we would live happily ever after.

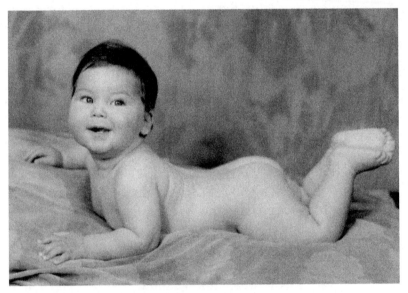

David, aged 6 months

Chapter 2

Early Years

How old were you? A couple of months? Yes, I guess that would be about right - for it would have been around this time that Derek discovered a lump in his testicle. This heralded anxious months involving an operation to remove the testicle, which had been diagnosed as cancerous. It is remarkable how human beings can cope under pressure, and certainly, at this time, there was more than a fair measure of worry. But you were a very good baby and gave us little trouble. You won't remember being hastily breast-fed and then passed to the care of my mother while I dashed off to catch a bus to the Good Hope Hospital, in Sutton Coldfield, where Derek was recovering from his operation. My mother often joked that she was surprised my milk was not the consistency of a milkshake, what with all the rushing about that I did.

Derek recovered after the cancer cells were removed, and despite his health problems your two brothers were born, eighteen months apart. It must have been hard for you to come to terms with two siblings following so soon from your own infancy – Ian a year later, then Michael. Babyhood finished very quickly for you and, perhaps because you were a physically large baby, you were expected to be a 'big boy'. Did we push you too hard? It is difficult to know looking back now, but it was a tough time for our family.

Despite an optimistic prognosis, Dad's health continued to be poor, and he underwent a further operation. He struggled, ultimately unsuccessfully, to keep his job, and life became tougher, with money in short supply. Amazingly, through it all, we remained a happy family, and I remember those days wistfully. Everything seemed much simpler, and we were bound by love and a determination to overcome our difficulties.

***

Back then playgroups were non-existent, and mothers had to entertain their own kids, which was fine as I loved playing with my little boys. Do you recall Kathleen who lived across the street? She was about the same age as you and you were good playmates, even though you insisted that 'cowboys and Indians' was the only game worth playing. You were always the good cowboy, with Kathleen your trusted ally.

I wish I could recall more of you as a young child, but memories blur, not least because of the many traumatic events in those years around Dad's illnesses. But one thing I do remember well was the close bond you had with Ian. This would grow steadily over the years and continue into adulthood.

Dad had not been well, and was now working away from home in London, returning to Birmingham at weekends to be with us, and travelling back to London on Sunday nights. The cancer had returned, and this time, due to a blood platelet deficiency, his chances of survival were considered slim. A blood transfusion was essential before he underwent radiotherapy, which was seen as his last chance.

I was beside myself with worry. I guess the first time you had an inkling that something was very wrong was when Dad returned to see us one weekend after having had radiation treatment which involved injecting massive doses of iodine through incisions in his feet. He had felt very unwell but, determined to be with us for the weekend, had driven back to

Birmingham on the point of collapse. He was in the bathroom when he started to haemorrhage from nose, ears and mouth. You had pushed the door open and, horrified, had rushed downstairs, throwing yourself at me and saying,

"Mummy, mummy I will look after you when Daddy's dead."

I will never forget the look on your face.

I recall how concerned your teacher was, as you seemed to shut off from all that had interested you and spent so much time staring into space. Communication between you and your school friends stopped. Why did it take me so long to understand what had happened? It was at the end of term parents' evening that your teacher, Mrs Couch, said she had tried to interest you in schoolwork but had concluded that you were just extremely stubborn. She had no idea of the problems we faced at home. Thirty years ago, cancer was a stigma. You certainly didn't go around telling people you had it.

It was amazing the difference when your teacher eventually knew the facts about Dad. She became a good friend, and, with her encouragement and gentle understanding, you began to blossom at school. It was a sad day when you had to change schools because we had to move house. Still, you did have Ian's companionship now, so the new school proved to be a happy and reasonably uneventful time for you.

***

We moved to a house nearby, in Sunnybank Road, and finally things seemed to be looking up. Dad had made a remarkable recovery; the massive doses of radiotherapy seemed to have successfully eliminated the cancer in his lymph glands.

Do you remember our large Labrador? He loved digging large holes in the centre of the lawn. We named him Ricky, after Dad's dog in South Africa in the early 1950s. I recall the romps in the snow in Sutton Park, and the slopes we would toboggan down in the winter. We imagined it was like living in Switzerland, and we were all so happy with our lovely house and our good friends.

Sadly, it was not to last. The publishing house, where Dad worked, was acquired and trouble hit us again. Dad was told he must move to Manchester with the company or lose his job. This was hard: I was not happy about moving North as I had lived most of my life in the Midlands and it was where my friends were. But we did, to a new house on a fast-developing housing estate in Hazel Grove, near Stockport. Thankfully, things proved far less difficult than I had feared, as everyone there came from other parts of the country and so the families bonded. You boys thought it was wonderful – like living on a campsite, complete with duckboards to get to the houses as the estate was still being built when we moved in.

For the kids, friendships came quickly, and you and your brothers soon teamed up with the Campbells: the 'gang' down the road. We hardly saw you boys; you were always out on the site doing what kids do: having adventures. The one 'adventure' Ian remembers vividly is the time you fell into a bog-like pit. It was a very dangerous situation as you were being sucked into quicksand-like mud and were unable to get out. Ian raced home to alert Dad who rushed to the site to save you. He placed planks across the mud and lay full-length on them to haul you out.

It was this event that Ian recalled years later when he stood at your bedside in February 1995, feeling once again that rush of helplessness and fear.

***

Those days in Hazel Grove were, I believe, happy ones for ten-year-old you. The companionship you shared with your brothers and the other children on the Torkington Park Estate seemed normal and stable. The school-run in the car, the friendships we adults enjoyed, helped to make the estate a special place where neighbours looked out for each other and there was a real community spirit.

It was around this point when Dad learnt that the Manchester office was to close and the whole operation was to be moved to London. This time there was no job offer for Dad, and he was made redundant. This led to our move to Australia, where my father's relations had emigrated in the 1920s.

Regretfully we left behind our friends in the North and said goodbye to our house in Hazel Grove, with its garden which Dad and I had lovingly planted and nurtured. I wonder, does the willow tree we planted still bloom at the bottom of the garden?

Australia – the land of Koala Bears and Kangaroos – awaited us, with all its uncertainties. And this time my mum came too. Nan, as you fondly called her, was a sprightly sixty-five-year-old who had decided to join us rather than live by herself in Manchester, where she had moved to be near us, or back in Birmingham, where she had previously lived since 1937.

Do you remember your eleventh birthday in the caravan park where we lived? Do you remember the fuzzy caterpillars that fell with a splosh in great clusters on the caravan roof? They were called 'Spitfires' because their spittle caused a stinging rash.

Eventually, despite all the upheavals, we did manage to find a house to rent in Eastwood, a suburb of Sydney, and Dad got a job with a publishing firm in the city. Nan also found work as a nursing orderly at North Ryde Hospital, and I began a degree course at Sydney University. But problems dogged us. Ian and Michael managed the change well, but you suffered merciless bullying at school. I often think that those days precipitated your problems in later life. An educational psychologist advised that you should learn to,

"Bully back. In Australia, you must do as we do."

What a nightmare those days were. You were prescribed Valium to help you sleep. You were assessed as academically very bright and above average intelligence, but you were not particularly 'sporty'. I guess this made you a natural victim of the bullies in a land where sport was so important. Your happiness did not improve, even when we changed schools. As a well-spoken English boy your personality did not go down well with your teacher, who was himself a bully. You could do nothing right by him so, if punishment was to be given, you were always first in line. Detentions, menial tasks, and even the cane were handed out for the smallest misdemeanour. It was Ian's class teacher who alerted us to the fact that you were being victimised and, dramatically, suggested the best remedy might be to leave not just the school but the country! God, the times I regret that we ever went there.

The decision came to a head when Nan had an operation for the removal of a cataract and, because the operation took place too soon, lost the sight in her right eye. Her left eye was also at risk but rather than go for this further operation she was advised to return to England. We would not allow her to travel back alone to an uncertain future, so it was decided we would all return. We weighed the pros and cons very carefully: your brothers were happy and had adjusted well to the Australian system, Dad had a steady job, and I was teaching, having passed my degree. Against this, my mother needed a solution to her eye problem, and you were very unhappy at school. I must admit too that I missed the culture of Britain. No amount of sea and sunshine could compensate.

David, aged five, at play with his brothers: Michael aged two, Ian aged four

David happily playing, aged eight

The Bickerton family clockwise from left to right (above) in 1973:
Ian, David aged 14, Derek, Cheryl (in Dorothea's arms), and Michael

In 1975 from left to right: Ian, Michael, Dorothea, Cheryl (in Derek's
arms), and David aged 16

Chapter 3

University years

Returning home was not without trauma, but eventually we settled in Surrey and past problems were outweighed by the fact that you were at last happy to have a place at the boys' County Grammar School, where you felt you belonged. I remember you saying,

"Thank you for getting me into this school. I am so happy now"

No more Valium, no more trips to the doctors or the educational psychologist. Your brothers too settled happily at the local primary school.

On the whole life seemed normal: Nan lived with us, and Dad found a job. And, although I did suffer injury in a car accident, I recovered to almost immediately find myself pregnant with your sister, Cheryl. We moved house to accommodate our growing family. I remember your bedroom – the floor covered with your toy soldiers and the many, many hours you and Ian spent waging wars and battles. A huge chunk of your early teenage years was spent playing soldiers. I sometimes look at those tiny miniature figures that you and Ian painted so painstakingly in authentic colours and regimental regalia. Academically, you had no problems and waltzed through your O- and A-levels; *"very artistic and talented"* came up time and again on your school reports. I have proud memories of watching your performance in *'A Man for All Seasons'* at school. You displayed talent as an actor, in addition to your work designing and making the set for the production.

***

University beckoned, and you were offered a place to study Art and Drama at the University of Wales, in Aberystwyth. You accepted, but after a couple of semesters moved to Reading University to read History of Art and German. From our visits to your room in the halls of residence at Reading, we had the impression you were settled and enjoying the course. But, at the end of your first year, we noticed a change in you. It was the beginning of the nightmare that would haunt us for the rest of our lives.

A 'chemical' breakdown was diagnosed, according to the university's Head of the Department. He added:

"When David has recovered, we will take him back."

I interpreted a 'chemical' breakdown as a 'mental' breakdown and spent hours debating what happened to you and why. Was it homesickness? It would be easy to blame your associates, but really David, I know the fault rested within you. Your dalliance with drugs and users – your enjoyment of drugs, the fake sense of confidence that drug use engenders – all of this made this artificial world more appealing to you. Eventually, it led to addiction to amphetamines, cocaine, and alcohol. We, your parents, were naive about the drug scene and there did not seem to be any help or advice available, so we just muddled along. We did what so many others did and still do: we denied the facts staring us in the face; we made excuses for anti-social behaviour on your part and, in the process, attempted to hide the truth from the rest of the world. The greatest tragedy was that we too were in denial; we were also hiding from the truth. We were totally unaware of the devastating results of drug use, but in the years that followed we would learn of them and pay the heavy price that drugs demanded, not just of you, but of your family.

***

Recently, Derek and I returned to the scene of your first holiday. We remembered the little toy car on the driveway of the Broadmark Hotel where we were staying at Rustington. We had taken a photograph of you sitting in the driving seat. Happy memories playing on the beach and in the warm sea, which you loved. We returned to Rustington the following year, this time with you, a boisterous toddler, and a very young Ian in tow. We loved the place and found such a relaxed and peaceful atmosphere there that we returned for a six-week stay when Dad was undergoing radiotherapy at the Royal Marsden Hospital, in Surrey. We felt Dad would enjoy the sea air, and we could all be together while he made his daily trips up to the hospital for treatment, then rest and recuperate in the rented house where we were staying. Trying to protect our children from the intense anxiety, the fear, and pain was difficult for Derek and me - the future was so full of doubt - but he was always so positive and determined to overcome his illness. His courage and faith helped me fight the fear, and so somehow we came through those dark days.

Years later, on our return to Rustington, sitting on the beach, bathed in glorious sunshine, the kindly ghosts of the past returned like loving spirits to soothe our sad hearts. Nothing can ever take away those memories.

Last night I thought deeply about whether I would be able to write about the next years of our lives, as we coped with addiction and its effects. This period is full of pain and fear. It is a good thing that we can only take life one day at a time, otherwise I do not believe we would have had the courage to endure the years of suffering that were to follow.

Chapter 4

Chemical breakdown

While we did our best to cope, lack of knowledge played a major role in our constant struggle with the unknown, and our inability to understand the true extent of your problems. Our GP prescribed tranquillisers and I assumed that these were for your 'nervous' breakdown because the symptoms you were displaying appeared to me to be very similar. Of course, none of us had ever dealt with a nervous breakdown and no one had explained to us the correct diagnosis, or the difference between that and a chemical breakdown. Sleeping all day and staying up all night, watching TV or whatever else you did in your bedroom, became your life, and the silence between us grew deeper. I called this 'the brick wall treatment': You on one side of the wall, the rest of us on the other.

I tried so hard not to let his unhappy state affect your sister, Cheryl, who was just eight. I remember how you would switch moods suddenly and without warning, fluctuating between relative calm when you wanted something – usually money – to being extremely aggressive. This led to rows over the most trivial of things, such as what to watch on TV. Your behaviour was very frightening for a small child, and while Cheryl would retreat in tears you appeared not to notice, nor care. Eventually, she stopped talking to you. More walls.

I became very worried about your eating. You had stopped joining us for meals, especially Sunday lunch which we had always eaten together as a family, and which was the focal point of the weekend. You remained in your room under your duvet. Many times, we set a place at the table for you, which stayed empty because you were 'asleep'. If you did join us, invariably it ended in an argument. In later years you told me how you hated Sunday lunch and the many rows that resulted from your behaviour. Your brothers said little, but I guess they felt exasperated by the attention your 'illness' seemed to warrant. They eventually left home so as not to be sucked into the pit into which we had sunk.

My lack of knowledge at that time meant that I was unaware that the use of stimulants (amphetamines, cocaine) would repress your appetite. Amphetamine use is linked with dieting and weight-loss, but results in aggressive mood swings. Why did we not seek help with your problem, which had now become *our* problem? It was not for lack of effort. I investigated every avenue I knew to find help. Even our neighbour, Val, tried to get advice for us, but to no avail.

The crunch came some years later when the tension in the house reached fever pitch. None of us spoke about 'the problem' because it always ended in bitter words which split the family. The slow, insidious advance of your addiction had reached yet another stage: Money was disappearing. At first, we did not notice loose change and small items of value going missing, like my cut-glass vases and silver fish knives and forks, but there was one day I will not forget. It still fills me with great sadness.

Cheryl was taking her ballet exam, and afterwards we were due to go away for a few days. My mother had died a couple of months previously, and her jewellery had been left to me in her will. Rather than leave these valuables in the house while we were away, I was going to place them in a bank deposit. Taking out her jewellery box I was stunned to find it almost empty. Cheryl walked into the room to find me sitting in a state of total shock and disbelief. I remember, even then, with the evidence staring me in the face, trying to recall whether I had placed the contents somewhere else and had forgotten where. Even then, David, I could not face the truth; I knew you loved my mother deeply and I could not believe that you would have stolen from her.

I went into your darkened bedroom where the curtains were permanently drawn. The mess was unbelievable: clothes on the floor, books, scraps of paper, cigarette butts and overflowing ashtrays, half-empty cups of cold coffee. You had wrapped yourself in permanent darkness. I will never know what made me pick up that scrap of crumpled paper from the mess on the floor. It was a pawnshop ticket for some of my mother's jewellery. I remember feeling sick and numb. I gave the ticket to Dad and left the matter in his hands because I just could not face the situation. Cheryl passed her ballet exam that day with honours, even though she too was distraught having seen me in such distress. I remember her childish rage that you could hurt us so much.

The whole messy business was dealt with by Dad, who managed to retrieve my mother's diamond ring from the pawnshop. Sadly, the rest of my mother's valuables and many items of my personal jewellery had already gone to pay for your drug habit. I guess it was at this point that we realised we had a serious problem that was not going to go away purely with kindness and understanding.

We took steps to safeguard our few remaining possessions and fitted locks on the bedroom doors. We now felt we had to urge you to seek specialist help. We decided to tell you that we would press charges for the theft of the jewellery *unless* you undertook a course of treatment. It was the wrong plan: Not only did we try to force you to seek help for all the wrong reasons, but more importantly, you were not ready to give up drug use. Oh David, how low you had fallen. Still, we clung to any glimmer of hope that things might improve.

Do you remember the endless middle of the night telephone calls from Jane? She was also studying at Reading University, where her ex-husband was your professor. I never understood the hold she had over you. A long-time drug addict, she was a woman of my age, with a son about your age. Her infatuation with you was an embarrassment to all who witnessed it, but what was it to you? I guess you were using her to get your drugs, or was it money? Maybe, you saw in this lonely, disturbed woman a reflection of your own vulnerability and loneliness? Whatever the reason, I never did get to the bottom of it, and I only know that for many months she would 'stalk' you with telephone calls at all hours of the day and night. On many occasions, there was only heavy breathing at the end of the line, but despite Dad's frustration and anger when answering the phone, she continued to call.

At this time, the few friends you had all used drugs.

"Normal people are so boring," you said.

One was a school friend, Steven, a very promising pupil, who dropped out. His parents then threw him out of the house as they could no longer cope with him. Steven drifted from one squat to another, and often turned up on our doorstep, on one occasion, barefoot in the pouring rain. Dad was so aghast that he offered him a pair of shoes, but Steven declined. Last I heard he was still heavily involved in drugs.

Chapter 5

A downward spiral

T he difficulties we had in coping with your 'Jekyll and Hyde' character made our lives a living hell. Your downwards spiral continued and there were fights – some violent – with Dad and your brothers. The endless arguments alternated with periods of total silence and lack of communication. I cannot believe that you enjoyed that miserable existence.

Today, I can write with knowledge that the path you took into addiction paradoxically blinds the drug user to the layers of self-loathing that drug use brings. We, your parents, were totally bewildered and could not understand why the child we loved and cherished could do this to us. We might have resorted to the course of action taken by so many other parents facing the same dilemma, as in the case of your friend Steven. But we could not do that, although we did consider it many times and it resulted in many painful arguments within our family. I could not reject you out of fear of where this might lead you. I had visions of you lying in a gutter, starving and sick. Maybe being mugged in an alley by some dealer to whom you owed money, or of a slide into still heavier drug use and criminality.

These possibilities haunted me. Suddenly, I was in the firing line – my 'coddling' was making you worse, so should I throw you out for the sake of the rest of us? I felt like a tennis ball being hit from one side of the court to the other – the family on one side and you on the other. Nothing I thought or did seemed to be right. How could I reject you when you were so alone and confused? I hated, yet loved you; I resented, yet cherished you. Some called it weakness; some called it stupidity. Families Anonymous, a group set up to support families of drug users, would call my attitude 'enabling'. However, I was not yet ready to let go. The result was devastating, as the poem I wrote at this time recalls:

Twisting in the heart an inky serpent.

Hope dodges from thought to thought

Looking for an outlet.

Please do not let this be.

Fears rise like fumes from the cauldron

Billowing out – shrouding everything.

Let go?

Who will catch the pieces?

Who will nurse the bruises?

Who will cradle the head – kiss it better?

LET GO ...

Ah, there lies the agony –

Love – not easy – always painful

You clutch your teddy bear – I turn away ...

The wall is built – darkness engulfs you ...

I see you no more.

I had fallen into a black pit of despair and found it hard to cope with the infants in my care at the pre-school playgroup where

I now worked. I was fortunate in having a wonderful and loyal team around me who, although not sure how to support me at this time, were also deeply shocked by what was happening to you. One of them suggested that I might find it helpful to visit the small chapel at the local catholic church, which remained open all day as a quiet place for prayer. I decided to go there after work, at lunchtime.

The chapel was indeed a peaceful and calming place, and the quiet was comforting. I found myself alone there and my prayers turned to an agony of tears. At first, I did not notice the little old lady but she, seeing my obvious distress, approached me to ask if she might get the priest to come and speak with me. I told her I was not a Catholic but that I needed to unload some of my pain. She asked me if I would like a cup of tea and would perhaps like to talk to her. I was so grateful for her kindness. When she returned with the tea, she sat and listened while I told her about you, and the problems we were facing. She asked me if I had a mother and I told her that, sadly, my mother had died about a year ago and I missed her terribly. She told me that the Virgin Mary would hear my prayers and look after me and my family, including you, David. She then asked me to return to the chapel at lunch time the next day and she would give me a small bottle of holy water to sprinkle around your room. Her words were a great comfort to me, and I left the chapel in a far healthier frame of mind after our talk. I must admit though to having doubts about the holy water!

I decided to return the next day to see her and to thank her for her kindness. I waited and prayed in the empty chapel until long after lunchtime, but my friendly old lady did not come. I decided to pop into the community centre across the courtyard to see if she was there. The caretaker, sweeping the path, was a middle-aged man. I asked him if he knew the white-haired, elderly lady who came to me in the chapel yesterday, dressed in a floral overall and wearing carpet slippers. He gave me an odd look and said he had no idea who I was talking about. However, he did ask inside the centre if anyone had brought a cup of tea to me in the chapel the day before, but no one had. I called into the chapel several times over the next few weeks, but I never saw my old lady. I did find my visits gave me a sense of peace and I lit candles and prayed for a cure from addiction for you.

Some years later and quite by chance I spoke to a friend about the old lady in the chapel. I was told that the previous priest at that Church had moved on, but he had, during his ministry, had a housekeeper who answered my description of the white-haired old lady. She had died from a heart attack about three years before the priest left the parish. Was she my friendly ghost who was such a comfort when I was so frightened and in such despair?

Sadly, pain and hurt, fear and hopelessness take over one's thinking. Love finds it impossible to survive. It's hard to believe that, eventually perhaps, there will come a happy solution, and all will be well once more. But tragically, a drug user must hit rock bottom before that has a chance of happening – and even then, there are no guarantees as to the outcome. Is rock bottom only applicable to the drug user? What about the other victims who are carried along in their wake? What about the family? What about their distress and fear?

Chapter 6

Family fallout

One terrible night Michael, your younger brother, discovered that you had taken his gold cufflinks. These had been a present from Nan, given to Michael on his twenty-first birthday, and they had once belonged to his grandfather. I believe that this was the final straw for Michael, and things were never again right between you from that day. Michael was furious, and you and he came to blows. It was a fearful fight, in which Dad also got involved. The front door was slammed shut and the top of your little finger was chopped almost clean off. Our next-door-neighbour took you to hospital to have it stitched.

Cheryl, who had been in bed, heard the noise from downstairs, and was terrified. I remember trying to soothe her back to sleep even though I was also deeply upset. The next morning, standing in the lounge with her hands on her hips, Cheryl said,

"What do you have to do to get attention in this house! Be a drug addict!"

Those words, from the mouth of a ten-year-old, cut right through me and I realised that I had become so absorbed in your problem that I had failed to see the emotional needs of the other members of my family. They deserved attention and understanding.

That night brought things to a head, and you too realised that the situation was untenable. You decided to leave home.

I recall following you round the house as you packed your few belongings. I felt such a sense of foreboding and fear. I felt I had failed miserably.

"Mum, why do you love me so much after all I have done to you? Forget me and get on with your own life."

These were your words. Words I will never forget and actions I knew I could never take. My faith in God had taken a considerable beating, but I prayed desperately for your well-being and that He would help you overcome your addiction. It was all that was left for me. My faith was one of the things that you would constantly throw back in my face, sneering and mocking me whenever we argued. You knew this was the one subject about which I could become enraged, and you used it to provoke me. But while it was always very hurtful for me, it must also have proved frustrating for you because nothing you could say could dislodge my faith. I knew that one day, in your time, you would have to come to terms with your own lack of faith if you were ever to gain the spiritual strength to overcome your addiction. However, this was not my major concern at that moment. All I could think of was the fact that you were leaving...

"Please David, when you feel you want to give up this way of life – come back to us. We will do everything possible to help you give up drugs. The door will always be open when you want to change."

I was so glad I said those words and did not simply shut the door on you forever. In hindsight, I often wonder what prompted me. It was as though someone else was speaking for me. I will never forget the sadness in your eyes. For a brief moment, I saw again the son I loved, the David I knew, before the dark veil again descended and a cold, indifferent stranger turned on his heel and left.

The depth of anguish I felt at this point is reflected in extracts from a letter I wrote to the Rt. Rev. David Shepherd, who was then Bishop of Liverpool. He had confirmed you into the Christian faith in December 1971.

'David cannot understand why I still care for him despite the many things he has done to hurt us. He cannot understand why I bother to help him and try to understand his addiction. Once or twice, I actually felt a warm response from him and an eagerness to explain his actions and then, quite suddenly, he would close up and an emotional brick wall would descend. This week the inevitable happened, and we had to ask David to leave our home. He has left, but to whom or where - I do not know.

He is unemployed, penniless, and now homeless. I have tried so hard to deal with the situation, but to no avail, and with a great emptiness I know there was no other solution. He had to go for the sake of the other family members. It is with this total despair that I write to you. I have given my son into God's keeping – my prayers for him and for all those like him will never end.

Please, My Lord Bishop, remember him. One of the last things he said to me was that he had to leave as he could not bear to hurt me anymore. I do not believe these words could have come from someone completely taken over by evil.'

The letter received a reply from the Bishop of Liverpool, and I will always cherish his words, which reflected his compassion and care for us at this dark time.

'I found it difficult to read your letter of 10 May because of the pain in it. How can I show my feelings for you? Please forgive my having taken so long to reply to a mother who is suffering the loss of her eldest son. But, Mrs Bickerton, you need no advice from me – your letter is dignified as well as deeply moving; you are entirely in command of yourself, and you have done everything as you should. I am filled with a sense of God's loving closeness to you as you describe what has happened, for on your cross, like Jesus in His despair and anguish, you commend yourself and yours to the omnipotent Father.

You are right – as you describe it, your son's illness has not conquered him entirely. In committing him to God, you have committed yourself too, and given Him your deepest trust. I shall remember you and your son, whom I confirmed, and your family in my prayers, as you ask me to, and I should greatly value you remembering me, Mrs. Bickerton, and all those who assist me, for you are very near to God.'

***

You would think the family now had the time to adjust to life without your menacing presence in the house. Peace and life without constant fights and rows! Dad decided that we needed to get away from it all, and so booked a short holiday in Greece.

I must be honest I cannot recall much of that break as I seemed to spend most of my time in limbo. Although we were only away for a week, to me it felt an eternity. My thoughts constantly wandered to where you might be, and I prayed that you were not deep in trouble. Not knowing what was happening to you was devastating, and I had no relief. I am sure that Dad also felt fear and concern but, like all true Brits, he kept a stiff upper lip. How difficult it must be for men to always maintain this 'strong' character, even though they are breaking inside.

It was Ian who told us that you had been in touch with him while we were away. You were having huge problems with Jane. It seems that you went to stay with her, after leaving us. The police had become involved, and Dad went to the police station to sort things out. You were so frightened and said you were finished with the drug scene. We were so pleased to hear this and said you could come home on the understanding that no drug use would be permitted.

Again, we were completely naïve to the ways in which addiction works. We gave you the task of painting the outside of our house, reasoning that this would keep you occupied so that you would not go seeking drugs. This was fine, and up to a point, we successfully saw you through a withdrawal. Sadly, what we had not understood was that coming off drugs was the easy part; staying off them was another matter. You began to drink heavily. However, it was not immediately apparent as a problem, and you seemed to be coping well with life. You were no longer the aggressive stranger among us. Relationships within the family improved, and you even began looking for your own flat and a job.

You were successful on both counts, and moved into a council flat, which we thought was a good move as it gave you a sense of responsibility for your own life. You found a job at the local library, which, although mundane, was a start for you and gave you the opportunity to become involved in local issues. It was not long before you became involved in a myriad of activities, which included running story sessions for the children at the library and handling issues which affected the residents of the estate, which, at that time, was a 'dumping ground' for dysfunctional families. Your interest and concern for those less fortunate than yourself became apparent, and you quickly became a valuable campaigner for better facilities and improvements on the estate. We were very optimistic for you. We were unaware of how your problem with alcohol was escalating.

Chapter 7

An attempt

Late one evening you appeared on our doorstep in a terrible state, covered from head to foot in green paint. You had walked from your flat to our house looking like an incredible green monster, your clothes covered in a thick, sticky slime! Do you remember sitting in the bath trying to remove the mess which coated your hair, your arms and your legs and your face? Afterwards, the bath had a semi-permanent green rim around it that took a great deal of scrubbing and elbow grease to remove. Your clothes were a write-off.

The story was that 'friends', who had been drinking and possibly using drugs too, had decided to 're-decorate' your flat with the artist's paint you had been given as a birthday present. They did not stop at painting your furniture, walls, and you, but completed the prank by tipping the remains of the paint out of your window. You had a sixth floor flat and so the paint splattered lines of washing hanging on balconies below and even the cars parked on the driveway.

I had given you the complete package of artist's equipment as a birthday present in the hope of renewing your artistic interest. You had shown such promise as an artist, and I hated that your talent should go to waste. I never envisaged that this present would be used in such a moronic way, and it hurt. You were so angry with these so-called friends that you wanted to take a hatchet to them. You had obviously been drinking heavily, and we had great difficulty dissuading you from this line of action.

Unsurprisingly, it was not long after this episode that you gave up this flat and returned to live with us at home. Your alcohol consumption had increased to the point where you could no longer cope and your interest in your work at the library, which had been so productive up to this point, waned. You handed in your notice.

Again, we were plunged into the devastating world of your addiction. There is always a price to pay for addiction and in the case of your alcohol problem it was not long before you were suffering its aftermath: depression. Your life revolved around your darkened bedroom where you spent most daylight hours under the duvet hiding from the world and, I guess, your own sense of failure.

This time, all of us living with you were frustrated and angry. Each coped in different ways: Dad tried to detach by blocking it out with work; Cheryl, now at secondary school, buried herself in new-found friendships and school; I tried to ignore the problem by continuing my part-time work running the Methodist Church playgroup. Each of us was exhausted and helpless. Returning home from work each day was like walking back into prison. The silence and the darkness were chains that bound me to an evil from which there seemed no escape. You had become the stranger in our house, the skeleton in our closet. We told no one of our plight, and we tried to live our lives around your dark presence.

It was easier for Michael and Ian. Michael was engaged to be married. He was busy with the preparations, and with decorating his flat where he was now living. Ian was living away with friends, and both boys were working and building their lives. They did not have to handle our problem on a day-to-day basis. At that time, Dad was travelling with his work, which meant Cheryl and I were sometimes on our own while Dad made overnight stays in various towns.

Once, when he was away staying in Paignton for a couple of days, I had returned from work as usual at lunchtime to the familiar situation. There was no sign of you, as you were in your bedroom, presumably asleep. I remember feeling particularly irritated that day at the thought that everyone else in the family was busy working and getting their lives together while you were hiding under your duvet. As the afternoon wore on, I decided to confront you and, if needs be, drag you out of your bed.

You opened your glazed eyes to look at me and said,

"Mum, please help me to finish it. Please, please put a pillow over my face and help me to die."

At first the truth did not dawn on me, but there on the floor by your bed were an empty bottle of Drambuie and an empty paracetamol bottle.

I remember sitting on your bed for what seemed an eternity, motionless, numb, and unable to think. I believe I tried to get you to talk to me and tell me when exactly you had taken the tablets. I tried to shake you, but you were heavy and limp, lapsing into unconsciousness. Everything seemed unreal, and even my movements seemed to be in slow motion. I left the room and was on my way to call 999 for an ambulance, but my legs gave way. I collapsed, trembling and useless. I really do not know how long I sat there on the stairs, but fortunately Michael had popped in to see me on his way back from a business call as he was aware that Dad was away. He quickly took matters in hand, calling our GP who told him to get you to hospital immediately. I still don't know how we managed to get you down the stairs and into Michael's small car.

The hospital took you straight through to the A&E department, as our GP had alerted them to expect us. It appears that the tablets you had taken earlier that morning had been in your system for several hours, long enough to cause damage to vital organs. It was unknown how many you had ingested because the Drambuie you had drunk had made you vomit. It was a grave situation. I could only sit and wait and pray.

While I remained at your bedside, Michael contacted Ian who rushed home to be with Cheryl who was now home from school. That evening we all debated whether to let Dad know what had happened. This was a difficult decision: Derek was a long way away in Devon. Was it fair to alert him into making a mad dash home to be with us? On the other hand, what if you died - what would Dad feel? Eventually Dad was told, but only after I knew that you had regained consciousness. We still did not know if there would be any complications from your overdose, but at least you were alive. Sitting in the hospital, my mind chased thoughts of guilt and anger that we still had not found the answer to your problem. I wrote this at 3am, waiting to know if you would live through the night:

"Help me to die"

That was your cry last night.

Despair filled my heart

With anguish – I could not answer you.

Waiting, waiting, waiting –

Why am I only human?

Lost for words –

Trying to build bridges where no land lies?

Making rafts of straw for you to clutch.

There is no easy way in life

Save by faith.

I know that.

When will you find it,

Dearest one?

Questions, questions, questions,

God, where are the answers?

Time to think, as minutes tick
Their endless toll.
Life flashed by – your life –
through the mirrors of my mind.
A kaleidoscope of incidents – some buried
So deep in the archives of memory,
I had forgotten their existence.
Your birth – that other time when
You and I struggled with pain.
The fates did not make that easy
or us either – did they, my son?
You came into the world shouting
protest – big and prickly – as you are now.

Last night we were alone again
With our pain –
Yours: despair ...
Mine: anguish.

YOU ARE NOT ALONE

Chapter 8

Rehabilitation

Y ou were discharged from hospital the very next day. We were dismayed; astonished that nothing appeared to have been decided regarding your mental state after the attempted suicide. It could be, of course, that you were offered help but declined it, wanting to come home instead. I will never know. What I did know was that I was very angry. I could not believe that you were the only person in the country suffering addiction and depression to the point of attempting suicide. I was determined to find some constructive help for you. But where?

Again, coincidence entered the scheme of things. I watched a television programme on addiction that week: *'Straight from the Horse's Mouth'*. I will never forget it because it was to prove a turning point in our lives. The programme told the story of actor Joss Ackland's son Paul, who had died of a drug overdose. It mentioned the Ackland family's involvement with a treatment centre in Devon. I wrote to Rosemary Ackland, Joss' wife, explaining our plight. This was to be the start of a friendship by mail that has now spanned many years. Rosemary rang me almost at once and recommended that we contact Broadreach House Treatment Centre in Plymouth and see if we could get you admitted there. We rang the centre to discover that, as it was a private treatment centre, the cost was more than we could afford. But the centre asked to speak to you directly, and there followed a lengthy telephone conversation between you and the admissions team.

At this time, you were drinking very heavily, and spending most of your time in bed in a drunken stupor, so I was very concerned that the Treatment Centre was talking to you at such length, knowing that you were not in a fit state to understand much of what was being said. But the result was surprising: Broadreach House agreed to offer you a place. They asked me to get you a one-way rail ticket to Plymouth for the following Monday morning. This we did with great trepidation. I was convinced you would never reach your destination safely. However, that evening a nurse at Broadreach House rang us to say you had arrived, completely drunk and somewhat the worse for wear, but that you were now safe and in their care. She advised us to stop worrying as you were no longer our problem, and that we should instead start looking after ourselves.

It was not easy to stop worrying and to let go of a problem that had become such a major part of our lives. Suddenly there was a yawning gap where worry had stood, and guilt stepped into the hole. While, gradually, we each felt as though a heavy weight had been lifted from our shoulders, at the same time we asked ourselves what right we had to feel unburdened and almost 'normal'? Thankfully, with time these feelings began to diminish. The sun returned to our lives for we knew you were in safe hands and, at last, we could relax.

About two weeks into your treatment, we received a phone call inviting us to visit you for a family therapy session. Dad and I drove down to Plymouth early that Sunday morning and arrived just after lunchtime. The group was made up of all the residents - 19 in total. Four chairs were placed in the centre of the circle of residents. You occupied one chair in the centre, while opposite you sat the group's facilitator. I remember her name was Barbara. Dad and I sat on the other two vacant chairs in the centre of the circle. We were totally unprepared for what was to follow.

Barbara began with a question:

"Tell me, David, how does it feel to try and turn your mother into a murderer?"

She was referring to your request for me to 'finish it all' when you took your overdose. While you said nothing, my reaction was of stunned shock. Barbara repeated the question several times, but still, you did not reply. She became quite exasperated at this point and said,

"If you want to commit suicide, why don't you walk out of here and into the main road where there is plenty of traffic – maybe a bus will run you over. I can promise you that no one here will get off their arse to save you."

Your face registered no emotion, but Dad and I were in floods of tears.

"Look what you are doing to your parents, David. What are you going to say to them?"

Your reply was a whisper,

"I'm sorry."

"Sorry? Sorry? Is that all you can say?" Barbara retorted. *"Well, group, what do we think of David?"*

At this point each member of the circle had a chance to make a comment,

"David, you're a bastard!"

"David you're a waste of space!"

"David you're scum!"

So it went on, until every member of the circle had voiced an opinion. I was crying uncontrollably, totally unable to understand what was to be gained from this brutal confrontation. Afterwards I spoke to your key worker, Anna, who was very kind and told us that you were very difficult and totally unresponsive to the gentle approach. You played 'games' in your counselling sessions and had built a facade which prevented you from gaining any benefit from the treatment. Broadreach felt that confrontation, although extremely painful, might be the only way to open you up and therefore address your problem. Anna explained that, until you accepted humility, and that the problem was of your own making, no progress could be achieved. The tough methods were used to break down your defences and, only when this happened, would you have a chance to begin your recovery. I still felt that this was a very harsh way to gain success, especially as you had attempted suicide only three weeks previously. I was deeply concerned because you did not say a word to us. I remember asking you how you felt. Your response chilled me to the bone:

"What does it matter? I have only one choice – to see this programme through or to go back on drugs and alcohol and die."

Nothing more was said, and Dad and I returned home, with me weeping for most of the journey. We both wanted to get as far away from Plymouth as possible. I had grave doubts that the treatment philosophy would work.

***

Our disturbing experience, and our expectation as a result that you might phone us any day to say you were leaving Plymouth, created fresh anxiety, and the shock and stress led me to develop pneumonia. So, when Broadreach House telephoned inviting us down the following weekend for another family session, I was too unwell to go, and Derek bravely made the trip alone. I admit to feeling a coward, deserting you and Dad in your moment of need, but maybe it was to prove a blessing in disguise. Dad needed to address his feelings and his relationship with you. I had adopted a protective role between father and son, on so many occasions trying to keep the peace between you two. Now you would be able to confront each other without my intervention.

I will never know exactly what transpired, but I believe you were at last able to relate positively to each other.

It was Mothering Sunday – an occasion you had always remembered by sending me a card. I was sad and worried knowing that the last time I saw you, you had been ice cold towards us. I did not know what to think, except to wonder if I had lost my beloved son.

The telephone rang at about 8.00pm that evening and it was you,

"Just to say mum, I haven't forgotten the day. I love you very much."

That was all you said, and remains a magical memory for I knew, at that moment, that my son had returned to me. It proved to be the start of your recovery from drug use. If I live to be a hundred, I will always cherish that day as it was the turning point not just for you, but for all of us who loved you. It is difficult to describe the resurgence of hope and the joy it gave me to know that you were at last successfully fighting your drug problem.

***

Your stay at Broadreach progressed and, although there remained many difficult and painful steps, you were now in a far stronger and more determined frame of mind to face them positively. I have often spoken of your time at Broadreach to other family members whose loved ones have been struggling with similar problems. I have told them how painful and humiliating the sessions were for us, but that, with courage, it is possible to overcome the difficulties, to survive and to recover, and above all, to learn so much about oneself as well as about their loved one. I have sent others to Broadreach since your time there, in the hope that they too will overcome their addictions. Sadly, not all have succeeded. Three found the treatment philosophy too difficult and walked away to return to drug use. However, there have been others who accepted that they had a problem, who stuck at the treatment and are now fit and well, and leading successful lives. This fact gives me so much joy and proves my belief that for those who want it, there is life after drug misuse.

I know that you felt that you owed Broadreach House a debt for giving you back your life. After you left treatment, you were pleased to help in their fundraising programmes, promoting their work, and speaking warmly of the help you received through their care. I too, shall always be grateful to Broadreach for saving your life and returning you to us.

Chapter 9

A new way of thinking

Perhaps now is the point to reflect on what happened to us, your family; how, despite your addiction and the pain, the fear, and the anger it created, a new way of thinking was born in us. I felt that there must be some purpose to all this suffering. Maybe there was a way to help others facing similar plights; maybe, our experience and the way we came through it all might help others struggling and unable to see a way forward? My thoughts began to develop around the possibility of forming a family support group for the relatives of drug users. But how to go about it?

I began by speaking to John, the minister of the local United Reformed Church. He was very supportive of the idea, and it was arranged that we hold twice monthly meetings in the church hall. During our darkest days with you, John had always been supportive of us as a family, and he recognised that there was a real need for this type of help. At this stage, I knew very little about counselling and had only my personal experience to guide me. I felt that, if I was to run this group properly, I needed hands-on tuition. I turned to Janet Marsh, who ran a support project in nearby Epsom, and who had helped us when we were undergoing such trauma with you. Rosemary Ackland had put Janet in touch with us then and now, once more, Janet agreed to help by offering to attend each of our group meetings. So, with this encouragement, *Family Support Group for the Relatives of Drug Users* was born. Little did Dad or I imagine that it would be the start of something

41

that would grow to become a lifeline to drug users and their families in South London. It was our way to make something positive out of our personal experience, and for us too, it provided much personal healing and growth.

After your return from Broadreach, you settled into getting your life together. Your intelligence, ability, and determination, and your personal experience as an ex-drug user, led you towards counselling in the addiction field. You had so much to offer. You quickly progressed through various courses and found yourself on a variety of committees for drug agencies, including our own group which Dad and I had now established, and which was seeking charitable status.

We were so pleased for you when you became HIV Coordinator for Mid-Surrey Health Authority, a position for which you had studied hard. You now lived at home, and we began to feel that our problems were at last behind us. You were not long in this post before you were headhunted for a senior post at Terrence Higgins Trust[1], in London. It was frontline work with HIV positive clients, and a job that you felt would be far more challenging. At this point your brother Ian and his partner Lydia were flat hunting in London and when they found a lovely, bright, and airy flat in Kennington, South London, you moved in with them, which made travelling to work in central London a lot easier.

David, we thought, is now settled and happy doing a job which he really enjoys! We were thrilled for you and were sure you had fallen on your feet. We finally felt able to relax and give our own work our full attention. I was finding it difficult to combine my work at the Methodist Church playgroup with the increasing demands of the group, due to its rapid growth. We were receiving more and more phone calls asking for help and, in fact, the needs of the group were taking over our lives. So, I

---

[1] Terrence Higgins Trust: https://www.tht.org.uk/ the UK's leading HIV and sexual health charity.

gave up my teaching to work full-time with the group, and to take counselling courses in the field of addiction.

David in Kennington in 1980

(photo: Lydia van der Meer)

YOU ARE NOT ALONE

Chapter 10

Heartbreak

Y ou too were working very hard at THT, setting up and developing a range of groups within the organisation, in addition to working with drug users who were diagnosed HIV positive. The demanding work totally enveloped you. To relieve the stress, you began to frequent gay bars and the club scene. Your behaviour started to change too. You were again drinking to cope with the stress and demands of your work and to keep up with your new friends and their way of life. Ian and Lydia became increasingly worried that you were going off the rails. You began to bring home friends who you had met at gay bars and who behaved in totally outrageous ways. Things reached a head when Ian and Lydia, returning from holiday, found one of these young men had moved in with you. You were obsessed with this young man, Mark, and were lavishing gifts and money on him. You were in the throes of your first love affair and completely vulnerable. Mark took full advantage and, when he had taken all that he wanted, dumped you. You bore the brutal consequences, emotionally and financially. You turned to heavier drinking and suffered severe depression.

I wonder how you felt when you saw Ian and Lydia so happy together. You too longed for such happiness. Mark must have seemed the answer to your prayers. Not long ago, I spoke to Ian about that time and asked him what he thought motivated you to be so self-destructive. He thought that you were never sure of yourself, even though you came across as a very

45

confident person. You found it hard to relate to others, particularly if you did not know them well. Loneliness played a major part. Having found a partner – something you had so longed for – only to end up being used and abused by him, must have been a terribly cruel blow.

I don't believe that you ever had problems accepting your own sexuality. It was the lack of understanding from others that you found difficult to deal with. It is heart-breaking for me to know that you never found true love and so never enjoyed happiness in a relationship. I have often thought that, had this happened, you might never have relapsed into addiction. But that now became the only way you could cope with the loss of your loved one, the loneliness and despair. As Ian said to me, it was a constant fight for you, even in the good times, for the devil of addiction was always on your shoulder waiting for you to slip.

It must have been a terrible shock for Ian to see you destroying yourself after all the years of suffering already behind you. Ian and Lydia kept these events from the rest of the family as they felt that Dad and I had already suffered enough and did not need this additional worry of your relapse. They hoped that you would pull out of it. Ian and Lydia coped as best they could, with you slowly sliding down into alcoholism, whilst still managing to carry on your work at THT.

***

It was some months later that matters came to a head. You were due to come home to us for Christmas, while Ian and Lydia were in Amsterdam with Lydia's family. On December 23rd, we got a phone call from you. You simply said,

"I'm calling to say goodbye."

You sounded calm and resigned. Your voice scared me. The dreadful realisation hit me that you were about to commit suicide. Shock was soon overtaken by an avalanche of helplessness knowing that we were at least an hour's drive away. Somehow, I had to keep you talking on the phone, but even now I cannot remember what was said. I knew that I had to get to you as quickly as possible, so I handed the phone to Cheryl and told her to keep you talking, while I got a neighbour to drive me from our home in Wallington to Kennington.

Arriving there, we discovered the shattering reality that we were too late to stop your suicide attempt – you were in the bath, your wrists slashed. We rushed you to the hospital.

Your broken love affair had triggered this episode. Ian told us how much you were drinking, and that you had also become a workaholic. You never did anything by halves! Everything you ever did was always to excess – even loving someone. You had given Mark, your lover, so much – squandering money and lavishing presents on him and dining out in expensive restaurants. Whatever Mark wanted, he got. As a result, you had spent money you didn't have, and used credit cards way beyond your means, trying to live a dream that was not to be. Mark flitted from lover to lover, taking everything as he went but giving nothing in return. After a terrible night in hospital, we brought you home, a crumbling, heartbroken mess. Christmas was not a happy time for us that year.

***

Understandably, Ian and Lydia had had enough of your behaviour and were looking for a flat of their own. They could not bear the way you were devastating their lives, and who can blame them? If you wished to ruin your life, then so be it, but you had no right to ruin theirs as well.

You were now on your own and determined to continue living in the Kennington flat as it was easy commuting to your work from there. Again, you poured your energies into your work, which became more and more demanding. Every day you were dealing with sick and dying young people. There was little supervision or support for you. Emotionally, it was taking a heavy toll and your drinking worsened. You even tried to get back with Mark and brought him over for a meal at our house. Mark was exactly as we had envisaged – young and good-looking, but of little substance. He had a hell of a high opinion of himself, and you worshipped him adoringly. It was such a sad occasion, and these were difficult days for us, as we tried to help you and understand the emotional turmoil you were suffering. Struggling and surviving was the sum of our existence. The situation was unbearable, but somehow, we lived through it.

Chapter 11

In turmoil

This seems a very one-sided narrative. It is impossible for me to express the inner turmoil you felt, David. Your own words, from your diaries, reveal so much about your heartbreak:

'How can you tell if someone

really cares for you,

if they never say so?

How do you know if

your feelings are misplaced,

if they aren't returned?

Can a friendship survive with just one side,

where the other lies so deeply

concealed, that it never expresses itself?

My head hurts,

as I contemplate the page, hurt

and confused.

Am I smashing my face into a wall?

How do I overcome this

overwhelming reticence,

49

this belief that callousness is affection -
the desperation of having nothing else?
What is there to hear if
nothing is ever said?
The groundless doubts that enter,
and weaken my sincerity,
the endless times I have to turn away
and be patient.'

And later.......

'After a while, perhaps I ought to commit my
thoughts to writing. I don't feel the intensity of
love I used to, but at times, like now, when I am on
my own, I do need you. Maybe it doesn't mean
much, selfishness personified. I have left you to
your own means, you will find your form of
contentment without me. But occasionally – not
often – I wish you were here. I'm wrong in loving
you – I say "loving" because that is the only way
I can express myself ...'

The words scream at me from the page, and my eyes fill with
tears. Oh David, forgive me if I am prying into what was your
private hell. Your writings give such a clear picture of the
sensitive man who was my son. I feel your spirit radiating from

the page, and this, in some strange way, gives me a feeling of your very closeness.

I guessed long before you told me that you were homosexual. And I knew that it would – as it did – bring you great pain and loneliness, due to society's difficulty in accepting such things. The world can be a very cruel place, and there is much prejudice and ignorance to overcome. Your sexual choice was your choice and accepting it was never a problem for me. I believe that your sexuality gave you a very compassionate understanding of the emotional needs of others, particularly women. I often saw this at work with those you helped through the group. You displayed an endless capacity to listen sympathetically to others – never judging, always caring. If you had never suffered yourself, you would never have had the experience to become such a brilliant counsellor.

Again, I quote from your diary. It seems as if you are looking fearfully at the ravages of your addiction on your physical appearance:

'The fingers feel the lines
– they prod the spaces –
Your ageing face
– the face that was once so beautiful is still there,
but unrecognisable – private hell.

Closer, then closer, you see yourself –
a mirrored image of what
you wanted to be.
As each day goes by – a little more –
you can't remember what it was
you wanted anyway.'

Eventually, the stress of your emotional pain and the heavy demands of your work at THT took their toll. Living in Kennington, virtually alone, with no support other than from the bottom of a glass, you reached the point where you could no longer carry on.

Chapter 12

Lost

W e brought you home, and you gave up the tenancy of your flat. Dad and I returned to clean the place up and sort out the final arrangements. Again, we as a family fell into the black hole. Suicide was an ever-present threat, but we lived from moment to moment in the hope that we would find some answers to our questions. It was obvious now that alcohol was merely a sticking plaster on a wound. The cause lay in deep-rooted emotional problems, and it would only be by confronting those problems that the addiction could be overcome. Colleagues from THT came to the rescue, and it was through their valuable support and expertise that we began to formulate a plan of action. You were, by now, seriously ill. All our attempts to find local help proved unacceptable to you as you had little faith in the 'system'. Eventually, with the help of the Minister from the local church, we arranged for your admission to a treatment centre in Hazelmere, Surrey.

THT was deeply sorry that the demands of your work had contributed to your breakdown, but they showed how much they valued and missed you by leaving the door open for you to return to work, when you regained your health.

My feelings then? Well, here is an extract from my diary:

Today has come and now is half over – I just can't

get it together. David slept most of the day – only

waking around 1.30pm to tell me he was frightened. Rhade, one of his colleagues from THT was due to come and see him and he was pinning so much hope on what she might advise.

"Mum, she is one of the best drug's workers in the country," you said.

It was then that I saw the bottle of Jack Daniels half hidden under your bed. Maybe this was a way to gradually detox you, David, by watering down the wretched whisky while you slept. How miserable and furtive I felt doing this!

He also dropped another thunderbolt: he had been injecting cocaine. He was crying when he told me, and I honestly believe he really did not want to do it. God knows what drives him to do so. He is so confused, unable to cope, and I find it harder and harder to keep a calm exterior. My heart breaks every time I look at him. It is appalling all this suffering! Oh God, please help me not to pin too many hopes on Rhade's visit.

I am not looking forward to the weekend. I dread what it might hold. Cheryl has her play this Sunday and will be rehearsing most of the time - at least it will keep her away from this trauma. I must try and get to the shops to buy Joseph (our grandson) a birthday present – I managed to ice a

birthday cake for him today. It was good therapy,
and I am pleased to say that the cake baked well.
I do not feel I can write more today – perhaps I
am too tired – it has been a hard day, but I must
keep going!

Reading this extract once more, I realise just how much I too had become a split personality. On the one hand your desperate mother, and on the other the automatic robot who went about her normal tasks presenting a calm exterior to the rest of the world.

I know my faith was taking a severe hammering. By now we had endured nine years of almost continual drug and alcohol misuse yet still there did not seem to be a light at the end of the tunnel. How we prayed for a miracle, or at least a sign to say we were on the right track!

More of your poetry written around this dark time:

'*Rain traces patterns,*
a translucent veil descending glass,
Red neon illuminates, penetrating,
cutting through the dimly lit room.
A fedora, with a bullet in the corpse
lying next to it.
The blood arranged in deliberation.
The deepest sense of defeat often
lessens the second time around.
Until it seems so natural to never win.
Prussian blue night sky, dawning,

as the final cigarette is drawn.

Quietly, the simplest movement

of a revolver to the head,

deep amongst the safe net

of the tree's distorted shadows.'

It was a bit like falling into the rabbit hole in *'Alice in Wonderland'* – never reaching the bottom and perpetually falling into inky blackness – terrified by the uncertainty. Unable to plan, unable to forget.

Chapter 13

No hope day

Your time at Hazelmere was therapeutic. I remember you saying that the therapy, based on the twelve-steps programme of Alcoholics Anonymous[2], although the same method used at Broadreach House, was not as intense or confrontational. The gentler pace was what you needed during your time at Hazelmere, which was a safe and supportive environment in which you could come to terms with the unhappiness and pain you had suffered over the last eighteen months. There was so much tragedy interwoven in your work at THT, given the many bereavements you witnessed. These were people you cared for, and you bore your grief without support. I have no doubt that this contributed to your relapse. You faced so many problems that I was not sure that six weeks at Hazelmere was long enough to satisfactorily tackle them. However, you successfully detoxed and returned to better health physically, if not yet mentally.

You decided not to return to THT and, in view of what had happened, this was a wise decision. You took a job at Greenwich Council Social Services Department, working with HIV/AIDS cases, devising care packages for them. This was a less stressful job, and you were full of enthusiasm and glad to be back at work.

---

[2] Alcoholics Anonymous

But a few months later things again went badly wrong. We received an urgent phone call from a hotel in Greenwich where you had passed out after another drinking binge. Dad came to the rescue, driving over there and endeavouring to sort things out with the hotel. You were in a very sorry state when he brought you home.

The reason why this had happened would leave us devastated. That day, David, you told us your awful secret. You had been diagnosed HIV positive.

No wonder your world came crashing down. My diary recounts my thoughts that day:

The most difficult part of loving someone is having to stand by and watch them suffer. Unable to bear the pain for them and share the burden of their despair – just being there with the knowledge that there is nothing you can do. Each one is locked in their personal little box of suffering to which must be added, in my case, the weight of helplessness that intensifies the despair. What is it that makes us mere humans so unable to cope? Animals find it much easier – the weakest of the litter is left out so that death comes quickly and mercifully. We humans feel the need to save a life whatever its quality. Something inside us does not allow for rejecting the misshapen, the terminally ill, or the weak, and yet, at times like today, I wonder if we are right, or whether it is just our own selfish

*needs to justify existence, or possessiveness that
stands between us and mercy.*

*Deep thoughts today, after a night wondering
what can be done that is positive and will get us
out of this rut we seem to have sunk into - drinking,
sleeping – the darkened room – dark as his soul –
depression eats into my very bones in the
oppressive silence.*

*Nothing happens, communication is at its lowest –
there is nothing to talk about so why waste the
effort to speak? The hunched shoulders tell the
story – the despair the withdrawn spirit suffers. I
am helpless and I really don't like it.*

***

A few weeks later, after you had undertaken further tests at St.
George's Hospital, we were bewildered to learn that your
results were negative. The hospital wanted to do a T-cell count
to confirm the outcome, but you were not willing to do so. It
felt like a game of Russian roulette with the HIV tests, and
apart from the consternation it caused us, the tests appeared
inconclusive. I wrote in my diary:

*We seem to have ordered our lives into little
pigeonholes – if David gives up drinking, then we
can deal with the T-cell count. If he doesn't, then
we can do nothing.*

Why is it that no one has thought about what all this is doing to you, David? Why is it that a person with the threat of this dreadful illness hanging over them, should be expected to be rational and act with good sense? They retorted that David, with all his experience and knowledge, should know better! Drinking only suppresses the immune system. The problem is: David does know. He has experienced the horrendous implications of holding in his arms a dying victim of this illness. It is this constant nightmare, and he is utterly afraid and without faith. The future is black, death is black, pain is black, disfigurement is black, time is black – this great yawning abyss is ever before his mind and there is no escape. What is alcohol but a brief solace, a temporary blotting out of reality, a space into which his tired, confused mind can escape? Away from reality for a few hours, before he surfaces, and it is time for another drink. Are we right to interfere? Have we the right?

The problem appeared insurmountable. It was impossible for others to comprehend. Friends tried to help, but to no avail. Others backed away, not knowing what to do or say. This was the blackest, most devastating time, and I recorded some of my thoughts in my diary:

Everywhere we turn there is this bureaucratic barrage of paper shuffling. All this way into civilisation, but still we insist on people conforming to patterns: "If he did this, we could do that"; "We could make an appointment next week". Go hang your heads in shame! The sands of time run out of the hourglass too quickly ...

On and on goes the terrible saga ...

Someday, dear diary, someone will say, "Yes, I know how she felt". However much you try there will never be enough tears to shed, enough despair to show just how I feel at this moment.
I cannot find words to tell you, but, maybe, just by writing this, I can begin to capture even a fragment of the moment when my world came tumbling down.
Coming to terms with the inevitable in all its starkness needs courage. I am fresh out of that so what do I do – weep? I have said there are not enough tears. So, the pain goes on behind this face a million demon thoughts flit in and out, leaving me motionless, speechless, numb.
My bastions of hope, faith, and love desert me and nothing matters anymore. Anger rallies a brief

flicker of activity within me, but quickly gives way to grief. Those pathetic words 'If only ...' creep back into focus and, just as quickly, I kick them out. Whatever is the use?

Today is 'No Hope Day' – a day to accept the burden is too big to handle. Thank you, world, I want to get off. Coming to terms with this ... I don't want to come to terms and behave in a rational way – I will leave all that to the professionals! Please, I want to scream and shout and vomit all my hurt – I can't go on ...

Oh David, what a terrible place to be, all of us, emotionally drained and helpless. You spent all your time in bed, under the duvet, with the curtains drawn so that day and night merged. We were desperate to know what we could do to help you.

Good friends came to visit and were brave enough to attempt to counsel you, but your response was always hostile. The hours they spent talking and trying to comfort you – so well-intentioned, but, ultimately, frustrating, and fruitless. Jackie, from THT, with her aromatherapy, warm friendship, and cuddles; Connie with her smiles, positive attitude, and skilled listening powers. Each tried so hard, but in the end accepted that it was for you alone to fight your way out and face life in all its reality.

I guess that you must have spent a great deal of thought and effort in fighting your demons and fears. All credit to you that after weeks of dark despair you made the supreme effort and arrived at a decision. You decided "to hell" with further tests and medical input! You would live your life with care, practise safer sex if the occasion arose, look after your health, and get on with your life. You told me,

"I have much to live for – my parents who I adore, and I also have a great deal of knowledge on this particular subject that might help others."

YOU ARE NOT ALONE

Chapter 14

Phoenix from the ashes

I believe you made the right decision and certainly the work you undertook from there on reflected this. You started work with Merton Voluntary Services as a Voluntary Agencies Community Worker. Your role was to liaise with the Social Services and Health Service in Merton, to foster a better working relationship and a clearer understanding of these statutory authorities among the voluntary organisations within the Borough. You also helped *Which* magazine produce a comprehensive guide for those affected by HIV/AIDS to receive appropriate support in the borough. Your talent helped establish many worthwhile schemes that have continued to develop, and which today involve a variety of voluntary agencies offering a range of help to so many people.

Our own agency was expanding too and outgrowing our home, with more and more people visiting us for help with drug problems. The frequent telephone calls took a heavy toll on our evenings and weekends. By now you were very interested in developing our group, and you played a significant role in obtaining grants from Comic Relief, which allowed us to move into premises in the local high street. As you took a more active part in running the operation, we began to expand in a professional way. We started a needle exchange and gained membership of SCODA (Standing Conference on Drug Abuse)[3].

How can I describe working with you? It was like trying to hold a meteor in your hand, knowing that it would leave you far behind when it moved. Your constant drive and energy left me gasping. It was impossible to keep up with you, and your demands upon yourself were relentless. You moved from one brilliant idea to the next, constantly pushing yourself, working at an exhausting pace, always speaking up for those who lacked your eloquence, and constantly confronting and challenging authority. You were never afraid to argue a point when you felt injustice had occurred, and at meetings many found you a prickly opponent.

The client work at Community Drug Helpline, as we were now called, increased considerably, and it is to your credit that many of these clients successfully conquered their addictions and got their lives back together. Indeed, some felt they owed their lives to you. I remember with pride one family that you helped. A family of four children: Perry, the eldest, had a severe cocaine addiction. He was seventeen and although not living at home, was constantly harassing his mother for money to pay dealers. He was often violent and abusive. His parents were separated. Father had an alcohol problem, but mother was a lovely, caring lady, close to a nervous breakdown, trying to make a little money go a long way and raise the three younger children – a girl of thirteen, who wanted to be a hairdresser, and the two youngest, aged four and two.

One day when she arrived at our office in great distress. Perry had called with his usual demands for money, and because she did not have any, he had picked up their small electric stove on which she did all her cooking and flung it against the wall, smashing it to pieces. She now had no means of cooking, and it was midwinter. Nor did she have money for food. You told

---

[3] SCODA was a 'national coordinating agency for voluntary organisations in the drugs field' between 1972 and 2000 https://wellcomecollection.org/works/vpjm6usy

me to stay with the mother and her small children while you went out. Within the hour you were back with a small portable electric cooker under your arm and a carrier bag with sandwiches and a few other groceries which you gave to this family.

Later that afternoon, I challenged you about this, saying we really could not take on Social Service's role with every distressed client who arrived at our door. Your reply was that you could not bear to think of those children going hungry, and anyway, you had paid for it out of your own pocket not from Community Drug Helpline funds. This was the first and last time I ever reproached you over ethics.

I know there were many others you helped in similar ways. Do you remember Toby who would buzz on our office front door after rolling out of the pub across the road? How many times did we tell him that we would not let him in, and we would not see him while he was drunk? This was almost impossible for him, as he was out of his mind from morning to night. Eventually, after a great deal of hard work, you did manage to get Social Services to agree to pay for Toby to enter Hazelmere for treatment. He came to see you just before he went in, and you had a very long counselling session in which he told you that you were the only person who gave him some self-esteem. Whatever the outcome of the treatment he would always hold you in the highest regard, and should he not survive despite all the help, he would put in a good word with God who, he was sure, worked through you, David, in this world. Toby had been studying to take Holy Orders in his earlier life, despite his alcohol problem. Tragically, Toby only stayed a short while in treatment. He came home and was found dead a week later. You were distraught.

There are so many other clients who loved and admired you. It was your empathy that made you such a good counsellor and which, combined with your wicked sense of humour, made you so approachable. You treated them like human beings not criminals, which was how society often saw them. You said:

67

"Behind every drug user beats a heart and a crying family."

The Mayors of Sutton and Merton with Dorothea at the opening of new
Community Drug Helpline premises, 1992

(photo: Lydia van der Meer)

Dorothea with special guests Pearl Carr and Teddy Johnson at the opening
of the new premises

(photo: Lydia van der Meer)

YOU ARE NOT ALONE

Chapter 15

Lost in Greece

In recounting the many cases in which your knowledge and compassion helped an individual and their family out of addiction and back into sobriety, it is not my aim to dwell on your countless achievements but to show how much of yourself you gave to the work.

You appeared happier in the company of a small group of friends, with whom you shared a love of films and books. You spent a fortune on books, so much so that bookshelves had to be erected on every wall in your bedroom, which quickly began to resemble a library. You also indulged your passion for designer label clothes. Your wardrobe swelled with expensive trousers and jackets, some of which you hardly ever wore. I think now that this may have been your way of disguising the fact that you hated yourself on the inside and so dressed up your appearance on the outside to compensate. I do not believe that I will ever comprehend how it was that you felt such self-hate when to me you were a strikingly good-looking, tall, blue-eyed man.

In June 1992, you decided to go on holiday in Greece. You had worked hard all year and had saved enough money. Dad and I were a little apprehensive that you were going on your own, but we hoped that you were by now sufficiently in charge of your life to manage. We agreed to pick you up from the airport when you returned in two weeks' time. That day we duly arrived at Gatwick and waited in the arrivals lounge for your flight. We waited anxiously as passengers passed through from the flight on which you were booked. But there was no sign of you. Dad made enquiries with the airport arrivals office and was told that your luggage had been checked in, but that you had failed to take the flight. You had been drinking and were refused permission to board the aircraft.

Dad and I were frantic. Where were you? We managed to collect your luggage from the airport, but there was no news of you or your whereabouts. So began a frantic round of telephone calls to travel agents, airport police, the Greek Embassy in Athens, and the airports in Gatwick and Thessaloniki (from where you were scheduled to fly home). It was to no avail: you had seemingly vanished from the face of the earth. We were sick with worry. Dad tried so hard to get information from the Greek airport, but with language difficulties it was impossible to make ourselves understood.

It was through the British Consulate in Salonica that Dad finally made a breakthrough. Alexia, one of the staff there, spoke good English, and made enquiries with the Greek airport. She was upset and surprised that they declined to give any information to her regarding David. It would be a further few days before Dad got a phone call from the British Embassy in Athens telling him that David had been admitted to a hospital in Salonica, and could we please make arrangements to collect him? We had no idea what state you might be in, and whether you would need an ambulance to transport you back to the UK. Apart from this, we were in no financial position to fund this trip. How grateful we were to Andy, one of your ex-clients. He insisted on helping us with Dad's airfare. Andy felt that he owed you his life, so this was the least he could do to help.

There were other complications, not least the difficulty in finding a flight for Dad, but we were lucky and managed to get a flight from Luton the next day. When Dad eventually reached the hospital, he found you on a metal-framed hammock in a corridor. You had no toiletries or change of clothes, as these had been packed in your baggage which had arrived at Gatwick, and your passport had been confiscated. You had been drinking heavily and needed drying-out before you could consider flying back to the UK. Dad somehow worked things through with the authorities and extricated you from this prison-like hospital. He spent a week nursing you back to health in a small hotel on the coast, after which he brought you home to England.

***

When you had sufficiently recovered, we talked about this episode. We asked you why you had felt the need to return to heavy drinking. You told us there were many reasons, not least that alcohol was cheap and readily available, but more importantly, that you were so very lonely. It was no fun being on holiday on your own. You had tried to pick up some Greek lads, but this had gone badly wrong. There were many blank periods in your memory. What happened between then and you ending up in a Greek hospital will always remain a mystery. It was about eight weeks after this 'holiday' before you felt fit enough to return to work.

YOU ARE NOT ALONE

Chapter 16

It all falls apart

I believe that being a parent is one of the hardest jobs in the world, and it only gets harder the older the children get. I can look back at the Greek episode and shudder at the mental trauma it cost Dad and me. I had nightmares about it for a long time afterwards, so I dread to think how it affected you. You must have been terrified and out of control. I know I felt that I would never again be able to let you go on holiday, or anywhere for that matter, without an escort, which was pretty silly as you were, to all intents and purposes, a grown man.

I remember, after your return to work I watched you very closely for signs of further problems and I realise now that it must have been around this time that you once more began to drink. Not heavily enough to affect your work or become drunk, but certainly to keep you going. It was strange that you were still able to work hard, deal with clients and operate so professionally at meetings. In all your dealings with people outside of the family circle, no one would have guessed that you were labouring under a heavy depression, reliant on alcohol to keep going.

The road back to alcoholism was slow and formidable. Try as I might, I was unable to get you to talk to me about it, and you continued to insist that nothing was wrong. Our relationship had grown closer through our work and at times there was an almost telepathic communication between us, particularly when dealing with clients. So many clients with whom we had worked together spoke of the amazing strength in our joint counselling sessions. We seemed able to block off so many of the avenues of escape in their arguments, both for the drug user and for their relatives. Between us we managed to cover the experience of both the user and the carer; we truly understood the emotional issues from both perspectives. We were like a pair of scissors, cutting to the truth; constructive, but often confrontational. Time and again we had successful outcomes. Clients gained new approaches to their individual problems and were able to accept our advice without feeling stigmatised.

In addition to work, I was so pleased that you enjoyed a social life mostly in the company of your good friend, Nathan, with whom you developed a strong and valuable friendship. You enjoyed your trips to the cinema and your shared love of music. These outings were perhaps among your happiest times, as you always seemed cheerful and full of fun when you were together, and even when Nathan introduced you to Janet, his partner, you continued to enjoy this friendship which was very important to you. There were certain other friendships that you enjoyed with female friends, but there was always this underlying thread of loneliness, which seemed to haunt you. You were always a good friend to have. You were a good listener and helped a great many of your friends through their emotional problems with your compassion, understanding, and, of course, a wicked sense of humour. Why was it that you could help others but were completely at a loss to help yourself?

***

Your relationship with Cheryl blossomed, and you displayed a protective and loving streak towards your little sister. She was now at university, and often telephoned seeking help about one project or another, usually to do with literature or film. You would busy yourself searching out the required information and spend time with her when she was home for the holidays.

The pain of the past relationship was repaired and there existed a strong and warm respect between you. This was another occasion when love proved to be the healing influence. Your relationship with your brothers too improved as they both valued your opinions and gradually drew you back into their lives, albeit cautiously.

For Derek and me it was different. We noticed that you were beginning to drink more heavily and eat less. Your days began to revolve around work, and you would return home late in the evening to eat and watch television, before retiring to bed. On weekends you would go out to the cinema, or to London to see Nathan. This pattern became your routine. I sensed you felt dissatisfied with life, particularly the fact that you lived at home with your parents when most young people had their own place. I watched you sink into melancholy which you tried to hide from me. I was too close to you not to be aware of this. I tried to get you to open-up but how many times did you tell me,

"Get off my back, mother."

You were a workaholic and, as a result, so many good things came from your efforts for Community Drug Helpline, including the opening of the needle exchange that you set up and ran, with the help of the outreach team from St. George's Hospital. This resulted in excellent working relationships and indeed friendships between us and the staff from the hospital. You became quite involved with this team, which used our premises twice a week for a clinic to offer outreach to drug users who needed prescriptions and specialist help around HIV/AIDS. Many evenings you spent talking to these clients in the waiting room and collecting urine specimens for Raj, the specialist team leader, who became a good friend.

You represented our charity on most meetings held throughout the Borough, including those involving the Health Authority and Social Services. You also attended meetings at national level concerning strategy around drug misuse, and you wrote papers on various elements of drug services for a wide variety of organisations all of whom held your opinion in high regard.

Why then, when you had so much going for you, did it all fall apart?

Chapter 17

The spark has gone

At times you would sit staring into space. It was as though you had detached yourself from your surroundings and were somewhere else. There was such sadness in your face, and even though these episodes were fleeting, I could not help but notice them. It was not long before you stopped talking to me, other than about work. You stopped talking about the future and denied me any access to your inner pain.

It was obvious to me that you were suffering, and my fears for you grew each day as I watched you become wearier, losing that spark you had brought to everything you did. You continued to turn on the charm and humour when you were with clients, always presenting your professional face. But the moment you were alone, down came the depression. I caught many glimpses of it during this period. You were such a good actor, able to fool everyone. But not me.

At the same time, you began to display physical signs of illness. Your face became inflamed and puffy, while your stomach began to swell, and your skin turned a sickly yellow. You suffered intense backache and pain in your joints, which you said must be rheumatism, and you had continual gastric troubles which you dosed with indigestion remedies, none of which helped. You refused to seek medical advice and did your best to hide these problems from us.

When Nathan and his partner Janet left Surrey to take up new jobs in the North, you sank further into depression. No longer did you look forward to Friday nights, which had been spent with Nathan, and you turned to heavier drinking and, often, your bed. Your alcohol intake increased alarmingly, and this had a serious impact on your fragile health. A deep depression took over and you stopped eating, replacing food with alcohol.

We struggled through until January when you came into the office one morning, barely able to walk, complaining of having difficulty in breathing. I promptly sent you home and Dad took you to the doctor. The advice was that you should stop drinking and let the doctor know how you were the following day. You went straight to bed on your return, but your symptoms gradually worsened over the next twenty-four hours until admission to hospital was unavoidable.

It is difficult to write about this time, loaded as it was with so much misgiving and worry, but I remember feeling glad that you had been admitted to hospital because I hoped that, at last, you might get the specialist help you so badly needed. I was single-handed at the office, with our administrator away on holiday and you ill, so I was not able to spend as much time as I would have liked visiting you. Cheryl had just completed a semester at university, and she decided to come home for the week that she had free. This proved so helpful to me as she was able to spend time with you at the hospital in my absence.

David, this is so hard for me. In retrospect, I wish with all my heart that I had closed the charity at this point and spent every waking hour at your bedside. Why, oh why, did I imagine that the needs of others were more important than those of my own son? But I know that at the time this was not how I thought. Back then, I really believed you were in good hands getting the medical help you needed.

***

Watching you slowly deteriorate on each of our visits and unable to find any solutions, left us very frustrated. Obviously, you were not getting alcohol, but your intake of all fluids had been limited to one jug of water per day. You seemed constantly thirsty and even though we attempted to moisten your lips with a wet flannel, you appeared to be in great discomfort. Dad tried to speak to the doctor on duty, but we were none the wiser as to the hospital's prognosis of your case. You were having a series of scans and a liver biopsy. There was talk of a liver transplant, but no other information was forthcoming from the medical staff.

At first, you seemed reasonably coherent, but after the first twenty-four hours in hospital, you began to be confused and little of what you said made sense. This was quickly followed by breathing difficulties for which you were placed on oxygen. Cheryl was with you most of the day and I came during the late afternoon. Between us, we attempted to keep the oxygen mask on which you kept pushing off your face. I brought a small blanket for you because your feet were so cold and swollen. I even cut the tops off your socks so that they were not restricting the blood supply to your feet due to the swelling.

Comfort was not a high priority in the ward, and the nurses seemed to spend their time dashing from one patient to the next. The other patients were very elderly and were suffering a variety of demanding ailments. You were the only young person on the ward, and there appeared to be the minimum of medical care for any of you, presumably due to a lack of staff. On one occasion, Dad and I rode up in the lift with the linen trolley which, when it arrived at your ward, was greeted with cheers from the nursing staff who confessed that they had had to resort to using bedspreads on the patients' beds as they had run out of sheets.

Several people visited you in hospital, including a good friend with many years of nursing experience who bullied you into eating a yoghurt as you were not eating any of the food presented to you by the hospital. I remember her coming to see me afterwards to tell me what a battle it had been.

***

You had been in hospital for five days when your condition deteriorated. It was a Saturday, and Cheryl and I spent the whole day with you. You had lapsed into a coma and all we could do was ensure that the oxygen mask remained on your face. The hours ticked by, and that evening Dad decided that we should go out and have a meal - the hospital would phone us if there was any change in your condition. Cheryl and I were very subdued, and I sensed that she, like me, feared the worst. That night we went to bed, and I remember praying hard, but with little hope in my heart.

It was no surprise when the phone rang at 3.45am on the morning of February 12. I tore down the stairs. It was the hospital asking us to come immediately. We dressed quickly, and Dad telephoned Ian and Michael. They would meet us at the hospital.

I will never forget seeing you with tubes attaching you to various monitors with their incessant beeping, nurses hovering over you, making adjustments. It seemed to me as though you, my beautiful son, were no longer there and they had replaced you with this immobile dummy. I fell on my knees beside your bed and took one of your hands. You were so cold.

I remembered one of our past conversations when you had told me how frightened you were of death. If there was a God, you were sure he would not want to know you because you had done so many terrible things. I remember saying that God was forgiving, and it was with these thoughts in my mind that I spoke to you softly - not to be afraid, I would hold your hand and talk you through the gates of death and, when the time came to let go, I would be there with you to pass you over into God's hands. I did not weep, I felt strong. I knew that this was the most precious task I would ever have to perform for my beloved son. I was wholly focused on you, David, and was totally oblivious to the others around your bed. As you came to me all those years ago, so I gave you back to God with all the love in my heart.

The family was stunned. I guess there is a numbness – nature's anaesthetic – which takes over the mind and body at that time. I cannot recall leaving the hospital, what the doctor said, or the drive home. But I do recall that it was a beautiful spring-like day, although early February. And so, I wrote:

As daylight awoke another day
you slipped away.
So silently, we
hardly noticed the
final whisper of breath
that said goodbye
to all the pain -
And so
your spirit left in peace -
quiet and beautiful -
just as we had prayed it would be.
Trolleys clattered; voices greeted
the morning.
nothing had changed for the rest of
the world
only for us, who cared for you so much,
the emptiness of life without you.

How can I describe my feelings that day? It was impossible to envisage carrying on without you. The importance and drive I had given to Community Drug Helpline seemed to slip away, leaving me drowning in despair and anger that so much of my time had been given to meeting the needs of other people at the expense of my own family. Everything seemed pointless. How could I hope to save others struggling with addictions but be completely inadequate when dealing with the problems of my own dear son?

***

The following week went by in a blur. Visiting the funeral parlour to say our farewells was traumatic. The body in the coffin did not seem to be you. It was cold and stiff and empty. Placing a kiss on your face and leaving a red rose with you, as we said our goodbyes, did nothing to ease the terrible pain and emptiness. I could not accept that this was so final. Death is not for those who have still so much to give and so much of their life left unfinished. Why should I live, while God has taken you? It was the wrong way round, and I could not accept it. I would have willingly given my life in exchange for yours.

At the funeral I finally broke. The sight of the hearse outside our home on that sunny February day turned my knees to jelly, and the tears and anguish blotted out everything.

It was a measure of the esteem in which you were held that so many attended that day: senior members of the teams from St. George's Hospital Centre for Addiction and Social Services, and dignitaries who had worked with you, some of whom who had become good friends. Nathan delivered a heartfelt address and spoke of your commitment and dedication to your work. He also spoke of your sense of fun and wicked sense of humour. You would be a great loss to the voluntary sector, but your many achievements in the field would be remembered. He then read a favourite poem of yours which had been on the wall above your desk at our office, *'Musée des Beaux Arts'* by W.H. Auden, the opening line of which reads,

"About suffering they were never wrong ..."

Strange, how I wished I could just be alone at this time so that my heart could break in private.

***

Many, many tributes arrived over the days that followed. So many people thought well of you and wanted to express their feelings. It was decided that a special fund should be set up in your name, under the charitable status of Community Drug Helpline: The David Bickerton Memorial Fund[4] would offer support at times of acute financial stress to families suffering as a result of substance abuse. The fund gave a helping hand to many people over the next five years, providing food, paying travel costs for treatment, and helping with clothing needs for children of drug users. I can imagine you smiling with satisfaction.

I must admit to having many doubts as to whether I could carry on the project and continue the work of Community Drug Helpline. I felt so inadequate without your help. However, something told me that I must not give up, otherwise the effort to set up CDH would have been pointless. I must fight on...

---

[4] The David Bickerton Memorial Fund still collects vital funds today and helps countless families in crisis. It is to this fund that all profits from this book will be donated. You can make further donations to this fund via the donate link on the website for the book: https://www.dbickerton.com

YOU ARE NOT ALONE

Chapter 18

We are not alone

To everyone's surprise, I returned to work just a few days after your funeral and threw myself in at the deep end with a couple of challenging cases. I still don't know how I managed to put my grief on hold while coping with other people's problems. Somehow, I felt your presence. Strangely, I was not alone with this feeling. Several clients who had known you, felt that I had turned a corner with my approach to counselling and I sometimes came out with words that rolled off my tongue as if you had spoken them. Gradually, I gathered strength in the knowledge that you were still 'sitting on my shoulder'. I became more confident and, I believe, a little more aggressive in my dealings with some organisations and in the wide variety of meetings I now had to attend in your place. It was as if your invisible presence was there to guide me. So, Community Drug Helpline did not fold, but continued to flourish.

In time, the project enlisted new volunteers and employees, which gave me the necessary support to continue. Our caseload increased, and new groups were formed, including a very successful weekly 'women-only' morning. I can look back now and see how these greater demands made me a stronger and more resilient person. There is no doubt that suffering can either destroy or strengthen a person. In my case it was the latter.

A couple of years later we received some money from Camelot, the UK National Lottery, and were able to train as auricular acupuncturists. This form of treatment has proved a very successful aid in the withdrawal from amphetamine and cocaine use. The course was very intensive and demanding. It entailed a week of working at the Gateway Clinic, treating a minimum of sixty patients. I am pleased to say that my colleagues from CDH and I all qualified.

We set up a clinic at CDH, and it was soon a thriving addition to the Project, with clients coming to us for treatment from all over the borough and further afield. This was one of the many new aspects of the work we undertook over the next few years.

It is good to recall that we also received our share of pats on the back for a job well done, including from Trust for London, which gave us funding in the early days of the Project. I was proud to attend a reception at London's Guildhall for voluntary organisations that had reached a ten-year goal and were still growing and successful. Dad came with me; I was pleased that he could share the moment. I felt your presence, and I knew that you would have been equally proud.

Although the continual pressure of work kept my mind busy, I was suffering and missing you every day, in every way.

My words on the first anniversary of your birthday:

> *My dreams came tumbling*
> *down like snow*
> *one day in February.*
> *It began in flurries sometime*
> *in October I recall.*
> *But the final avalanche engulfed,*
> *submerged, imprisoned completely.*
> *Numbing, drowning grief so deep*

it could not be overcome.
They say:
time heals –
the snow will melt
the sun will shine
healing will begin.
But not yet ... Not yet ...
Tears like ice – diamonds pierce my heart –
memory not yet born –
transfixed by pain to a hospital bed
in February.

On the first anniversary of your death I wrote,

Today I shed more tears than I thought possible and still I cry within my heart. The pain takes its unrelenting toll on all my being. I cannot think, save to cry for what is lost to me. How to survive and greet each day of this life with hope and eagerness. There is nothing I can do that will release me from the ache. Yet still, life's journey beckons and demands the forward trail. Leave behind what was yesterday's hope and move on – I wish that I could remain – but then nothing is forever – so maybe tomorrow's dust will be me.

It is strange how many times in life I have had occasion to feel your presence, and I am not alone in this feeling. Four years on, Cheryl had a launch party for her programme that was shown on Channel 4 called *'Fashion Victims'*. It was her debut as a director, and Dad and I were immensely proud. Such a happy occasion with so many old friends and new colleagues attending to give her support. After the broadcast, Cheryl came straight over to me and gave me a big hug and with tears in her eyes she said, what I already knew,

"David is here."

Derek also felt that you were with us at this marvellous moment in Cheryl's life.

***

I have spoken to Cheryl at length about that time and she wrote to me with an account of those final days.

Chapter 19

Cheryl's Recount

M um, you have asked me what I remember of the time David was in hospital. This is an incredibly difficult question for me to answer, not because I don't remember, but because I remember too clearly. I hope it's what you want to hear.

***

David hardly said anything during those few days - I talked for both of us, I think. Although I didn't want to admit it, I knew in my heart that it was the end and found myself talking as if it was the last chance I'd ever have. I didn't really know what to say but I hated the idea of sitting there saying nothing. So, I started telling him about my dreams, about my future. I wanted him to know that I was going to succeed and that it was for him that I would do it. I told him I was going to be a great actress and director and was going to train with Philippe Gaulier. I talked about films I had seen and loved, and he smiled in recognition. I wanted to let him know that he shouldn't worry about me. I wanted him to know that I was going to go out there and win. He heard me and he smiled as I spoke, but he said nothing. I could see he was in pain, and he wanted to think about other things, but I wouldn't let him, I just kept talking, hoping it would distract him.

In the first day or so he was always trying to sneak cigarettes, and I thought,

"What the hell. Why should I deprive him of something he enjoys?"

So, I bought him some ciggies, and helped him to sneak into the communal room to hang his head out of the window and smoke. I remember he was the loudest one on the ward during those days, teasing the old ladies in the other beds and cursing the nurses for moving him and hurting. He would interrupt my flow by shouting some teasing rebuke at the old lady across the way – he was the entertainer for a brief time, but then he slipped so quickly.

I think back now, and I realise that in truth we had no conversations. I talked and he listened, and I talked, and he gradually heard less, until I talked to a vacant face and found myself wondering if he heard anything at all. I remember thinking at the time,

"Why did it have to come to this for me to be able to tell you these things?"

Much of the time it felt like any other hospital visit – chatting inanely to fill the gaps and distract his attention. He said very little. I do remember him telling me what the doctors were doing to him and how the bags kept being changed as they filled up with drained green bile. He found it irritating and uncomfortable, but he seemed somehow resigned. I remember thinking, why aren't you fighting? You've got to fight this. Perhaps I thought that telling him about *my* determination would somehow spark *his*. The truth was, he had given up.

How do you convince someone who believes they have no reason to live that there is reason? When someone is inevitably dying, why stop them from making it happen sooner rather than later? Is it selfish to ask them to hold off, hang on, to stay with you?

"Find me a reason and I'll stop..."

"Change what has passed and I'll change my mind..."

To hold the hand that doesn't hold the knife –

To hold the head that should have hit the floor –

To remove the clothes that smother a floundering corpse.

I had reached a point where I could no longer deny the inevitable. I wished for a miracle cure – every minute of every day – but in my heart I guess I just wanted the pain to stop. It was a question all through the years that I came back to, again and again: Why?

No matter how much love came from his family, no matter how many people his inspiration touched, no matter what strength he gave to others, he could not save himself. He fought demons from within as he battled to find the love he sought – the real love that he believed would be the key to all happiness. Nothing I ever said convinced him that life was worth it. Nothing anyone ever said would.

A final burning memory:

A wave of blue washed over his head and, as the tides came in, he sank, unable to surface. The crests of the waves barely flickered in his eyes. Sinking under, the onlookers waited with bated breath for the next fighting gasp.

Again, it goes and we wonder, silently, if it will
come again.
Longer.
Much longer.

Then at last it comes: long, slow, sighing.
That's it.

No. Again –
A gasp and duck under –
Together, we hold our breath, expecting a final
surge.

The wave emerges, foaming.
Completely submerged.

I had heard that breath before: a sigh of exasperation, an exhausted release, an exclamation on a tiresome, pointless situation. He had simply had enough. For two days, I had been unable to recognise that ventilated, brain-dead corpse, yet, as that last foaming sigh was released, I found myself looking up and I saw David leaving.

The crest of a wave
Has always been your threshold
Riding high,
Drifting onward.

It has been your hand
I have reached to for salvation,

Drawing me back
From depths of depression.

Now your hand in ours,
We surround you, we carry you,
Keep your head above water,
Fight tides that drag you.

You seep through our fingers –
Do you not feel them around you?
Slipping out of the night,
Your little breath flickers.

Come up for air, sweetheart,
Don't fear the shadows;
Let the waves wash over you,
Cleanse you, dispense you.

Slide away to a far-away shore -
We will be with you,
Never to leave you;
You slip under for the last time.

The waves settle,
Nothing ripples perfection.
A solitary blue crest
Rides this white ocean.

Epilogue

S o, life goes on, and we continue to try and keep it all together. The initial raw pain of loss has eased a little. Or perhaps I have just found a way of coping. As one birthday follows another, and so too the anniversary of your death, we can look back and reflect.

I have spoken at many gatherings of organisations, and each time I am a little stronger and more positive in my outlook. I believe that the entire success of the work of Community Drug Helpline has been at a very personal level. As I have said many times, if our family had not experienced drug and alcohol addiction from its early stages right through to its bitter end how could we possibly empathise with the people who sought our help over the years? Love and compassion have been the foundation of all my work with clients and the major factor in helping them to learn to cope with their problems - be they a distraught relative seeking answers, or a chaotic drug user. This method of counselling has given them a feeling that they are not so alone. It has enabled them to find a new strength to fight the negative attitudes that have for so long been their lot in life.

To help relatives to a better understanding of drug misuse I wrote a simple leaflet, *A Positive Approach*[5] setting out the various stages of addiction and including some ideas for addressing the problems. I included the views of members of the family support group and some clients. It has been well received and has become a useful guide to those in need, both

---

[5] *A Positive Approach* is available to download from the website for this book:
https://www.dbickerton.com

in Community Drug Helpline and other organisations dealing with drug problems.

Last year, David, I felt it was time to hand over the reins. I had worked long and hard to place CDH on a firm financial footing. The employees and volunteers now working at the Project are well-trained and fully committed to its continued success. On a more personal level, I was now nearly 70 and at a stage when most have retired to a more sedate and peaceful life. However, the final decision came when Dad's heart problems gave grave cause for concern, and I realised that he needed one hundred percent of my time and care.

Nonetheless, it was not an easy decision. Community Drug Helpline was my baby and had been nurtured at a huge personal cost for 15 years. I still cannot quite believe that we had achieved so much for those suffering from addiction from the small seed of hope that we planted all those years ago. Despite all the frustrations and disappointments that we encountered, we battled on, undaunted. So much love, so much determination to succeed, and so much quiet satisfaction in our successes.

Dear David, I could never have achieved any of this without you. You were not only the inspiration behind the cause but were to become the formidable champion and senior player in the growth of the charity. Is it any wonder that I continued to feel your presence so strongly when making decisions at work, even though you had been gone five years? Oh yes, I shall miss the feeling of your closeness in this very special area of our work together. In a way it is a double-edged bereavement.

***

I completed one final task before I left CDH. Something I wondered if I would ever have the courage to complete. It was not without a great deal of pain that I wrote a short leaflet for use within the Project for those who have been bereaved as a result of drug addiction: *Coping with the Death of a Loved One*[6]. This leaflet has reached many sad homes, and I pray that it offers some small solace to ease the suffering.

I believe that I have grown through suffering and have become a wiser and more compassionate person. I also know that the skills I have learnt will continue to be a source of help to others for as long as I live. You too, did your share of suffering and still managed to give a huge measure of care to others. This is your living legacy and it will never be forgotten by those fortunate to have benefited from your help.

However, above all, you were my beloved son. I do not regret one moment of your life, the bad and the good days are pieces of the same kaleidoscope. This poem was written on October 31, 2000, what would have been your 42nd birthday. It comes to you with all my love.

What have I left of you on this, your birthday?

A heart full of love for you;

A box full of photographs;

A mind full of memories.

No grave to visit – just a spot

where ashes were scattered –

You have left that place – were you ever there?

You gave me your spirit to

strengthen me along life's way.

You gave the knowledge that you would

be with me for as long as I

continued to remember you.

---

[6] *Coping with the Death of a Loved One* is available to download from the website for this book: https://www.dbickerton.com

You have not gone far away,

but are just out of sight for a little while ...

David, I have done what I set out to do: to write with my heart what I never said to your face. Cheryl told me that I must never regret anything – and I don't. I was always there for you, especially in the dark days. She also felt that writing all this down would be good, not just for me, but for others who might empathise with what I had to say. Sharing your heart and mind is the greatest gift you can give, and there couldn't be a more worthy tribute to a wonderful, wonderful man. So, there we have it, dear son: my catharsis and your memorial. Rest in peace.

Today is shrouded in past times.

How fast flows the present into the unknown.

Yet, it is as nothing.

Today, memory is revisited, and all is still.

With lingering, loving care I stroke each thought.

Beyond the ravages of time –

You wait so patiently –

That warm beloved smile, so well-remembered.

Your whispered love surrounds us all.

We are content.

October 2003

YOU ARE NOT ALONE

YOU ARE NOT ALONE

The David Bickerton Memorial Fund

All profits from this book will be donated to the David Bickerton Memorial Fund, as mum and David would have wanted. The Fund is managed by CDARS (Community Drug and Alcohol Recovery Services), the name that Community Drug Helpline now goes by. Donations will help CDARS to carry on the benevolent work that David began: helping families in crisis by providing emergency essentials, from food to fridges. Your purchase of this book means that another family will not go without.

If you would like to make further donations to this charitable fund, you can find a link to the JustGiving page on our website: https://www.dbickerton.com or simply scan the QR code:

Appendix

The following are links to UK based organisations you may find useful if you, or anyone you know, is facing the agony of addiction. Scan the QR code to be taken to our 'useful contacts' page on our website, with direct links to all the agencies listed below:

Addiction Support

Community Drug and Alcohol Recovery Services (CDARS)

https://www.cdars.org.uk/

Crisis Helpline: 07944 506036 (24 hours a day, 7 days a week)

CDARS is the charity that Dorothea Bickerton founded in 1985. It flourishes today under this new title. Nearly 40 years on, CDARS leads the way in the field of addiction, being recognised as one of the top support agencies in the UK, helping over 1200 people each year by providing a variety of services designed to support vulnerable people with complex needs, including drug and alcohol misuse, mental health, neurodiversity, veterans, and perpetrators of domestic violence. CDARS upholds the same values upon which Dorothea built the organisation, with David at her side: people-centred, inclusive, respectful, non-judgemental, confidential, and holistic to the needs of the individual, providing support to improve the mental, physical, social, emotional health and well-being of the whole person.

FRANK

https://www.talktofrank.com

Call FRANK: 0300 123 6600 (24 hours a day, 7 days a week)
Text 82111
Email: https://www.talktofrank.com/contact

For anyone concerned for themselves, a family member or friend. Confidential advice and information about drugs, their effects, and the law. Useful A-Z reference with information about every drug. Find details of local and national services that provide counselling and treatment in England.

The National Addiction Treatment & Rehabilitation Directory

http://www.uk-rehab.com/

Helpline: 02038 115 619 (24 hours a day, 7 days a week)

The National Addiction Treatment & Rehabilitation Directory contains over 700 addiction treatment services, as well as an extensive directory of information about different types of addiction, drugs, alcohol, support services and therapies.

There's a free 24/7 call back service via the website.

Alcoholics Anonymous (AA)

https://www.alcoholics-anonymous.org.uk
National free helpline: 0800 9177 650
Email for support: help@aamail.org
The website also has a chat box.

AA provides help and support for anyone with alcohol problems. Alcoholics Anonymous is a fellowship of people who share their experience, strength and hope with each other to solve their common problem and help others to recover from alcoholism. There are local meetings all over the UK that can be found using the search function on the main website. AA is a global organisation and details of AA meetings around the world can be found here: https://www.aa.org/aa-around-the-world

Alcohol Change UK

https://alcoholchange.org.uk

A site that predominantly offers information and support options for people worried about how much alcohol they are drinking or those who are worried about someone else's drinking. Does not offer a helpline.

Cocaine Anonymous UK

https://www.cocaineanonymous.org.uk

CAUK helpline: 0800 612 0225 (10:00 to 22:00, 7 days a week)
Email CAUK: helpline@cauk.org.uk

Offering help and support for anyone who wants to stop using cocaine with regular local meetings held throughout England and Wales, as well as online.

Narcotics Anonymous

https://www.ukna.org

Helpline 0300 999 1212 (10:00-24:00, 7 days a week)
General email: pi@ukna.org
Email to enquire about meetings near you:
meetings@ukna.org

Narcotics Anonymous offers support for anyone in the UK & Channel Islands who wants to stop using drugs. If you have a problem, NA is run by recovering drug addicts who can help you get and stay clean.

Release

https://www.release.org.uk

Helpline: 020 7324 2989 (11:00-13:00 & 14:00-16:00, Monday to Friday. A message service is available 24 hours)
Email helpline: ask@release.org.uk

National charity that offers free and confidential advice about drugs and the law.

Samaritans

https://www.samaritans.org

Call: 116 123 - it's FREE (24 hours a day, 7 days a week)
Email: jo@samaritans.org.uk

Offering emotional support 24 hours a day for anything you are going through. There is an online chat available on the website and a self-help app. You can even write a Samaritan a letter:

Freepost SAMARITANS LETTERS

The Compassionate Friends

https://www.tcf.org.uk

0345 123 2304 – helpline (10:00 – 16:00 and 19:00 – 22:00, every day of the year)
helpline@tcf.org.uk

A charitable organisation of bereaved parents, siblings and grandparents dedicated to the support and care of other similarly bereaved family members who have suffered the death of a child or children of any age and from any cause.

Mind

www.mind.org.uk

Infoline: 0300 123 3393 (not free)
Legal line: 0300 466 6463 (not free)
Email: info@mind.org.uk

Mind offers extensive resources, information, advice and answers to questions about types of mental health problems, where to get help, drug and alternative treatments, advocacy.

National Suicide Prevention Helpline UK

https://www.spuk.org.uk/national-suicide-prevention-helpline-uk/

0800 689 5652 (18:00-03:30, 7 days a week)

Offers a supportive listening service to anyone with thoughts of suicide. The website provides useful information for anyone worried for themselves or someone else.

Mental Health Foundation

www.mentalhealth.org.uk

Mental Health Foundation is involved with research, advocacy and projects connected to mental health. They run a wide range of programmes covering families, young people, children, pregnancy, later life, refugees, poverty, Covid, workplace mental health and more. The website provides information about all aspects of mental health with a useful A-Z directory.

Shout

https://giveusashout.org

Text 'SHOUT' to 85258 (24 hours a day, 7 days a week)

Shout Crisis confidential text line for support in a crisis. A free service and messages will not appear on your phone bill. Responses are usually within 5 minutes.

If you're experiencing a personal crisis, are unable to cope and need support; if you're feeling low, anxious, worried, lonely, overwhelmed, suicidal or not quite yourself, Shout can help with urgent issues such as: suicidal thoughts; abuse or assault; self-harm; bullying; relationship challenges; anxiety; chronic pain; grief; depression; loneliness; sleep. The website provides useful resources on a range of life matters: autism; cost of living; Covid; social media; eating disorders; LGBTQ+; student life and more.

CALM – Campaign Against Living Miserably

https://www.thecalmzone.net/get-support

Call 0800 58 58 58 (17:00-24:00 – 365 days a year)
Webchat via the website (17:00-24:00 – 365 days a year)

The Campaign Against Living Miserably (CALM) is leading a movement against suicide. You can talk to CALM about anything. Offering an A-Z directory of guides on a vast range of issues, such as abuse; addiction; anger; bipolar disorder; body image and many more.

Papyrus HOPELINEUK

https://www.papyrus-uk.org

HOPELINEUK - 0800 068 4141 (weekdays 10:00-22:00, weekends 14:00-22:00)
Email pat@papyrus-uk.org
Text 07786 209 697.

If you're under 35 and struggling with suicidal feelings or concerned about a young person who might be struggling, contact Papyrus.

Rethink Mental Illness

https://www.rethink.org

Advice and information helpline: 0808 801 0525 (09:30-16:00, Monday to Friday, excluding bank holidays)
Webchat service (10:00-13:00, Monday to Friday, excluding bank holidays)
Email advice@rethink.org (response within 3 working days)
Write to: Rethink, PO BOX 18252 Solihull B91 9BA
(response posted within 3 working days)

Advice and information line for practical advice on: types of therapy and medication; benefits, debt, money issues; police, courts, prison; your rights under the Mental Health Act.

Nightline

https://nightline.ac.uk

Nightline offers a unique listening service, providing emotional support and information to students across the country. It's the only service of its kind dedicated to students in higher and further education. Run by students, our listening volunteers ensure every student can talk about their feelings in a safe, non-judgemental environment. If you're a student, you can look on the Nightline website to see if your university or college offers a night-time listening service. Nightline phone operators are all students too.

Switchboard LGBT+ Helpline

https://switchboard.lgbt

LGBT+ helpline - 0800 0119 100 (10:00-22:00 every day) Email chris@switchboard.lgbt

If you identify as gay, lesbian, bisexual or transgender, you can contact Switchboard or use the webchat service. Phone operators all identify as LGBT+.

National Autistic Society

www.autism.org.uk

UKs leading charity for *autistic* people and their families. Website provides useful information, advice, educational resources, as well as information about mental health and addiction.

The ADHD Foundation Neurodiversity Charity

https://www.adhdfoundation.org.uk

The ADHD Foundation Neurodiversity Charity advocates for and actively improves the life chances of those living with and impacted by ADHD, Autism, dyslexia, dyspraxia (DCD), Tourette's syndrome, dyscalculia, dysgraphia, and any related physical and psychological health concerns. Website provides information, advice, education, training, screening clinic and further support.

Citizens Advice Bureau

https://www.citizensadvice.org.uk

For advice about benefits, debt problems, legal issues, housing, health and local services. The Citizens Advice Bureau website has a directory listing its local offices.

Hub of Hope

https://hubofhope.co.uk

The Hub of Hope is the UK's leading mental health support database. It is provided by national mental health charity, Chasing the Stigma, and brings local, national, peer, community, charity, private and NHS mental health support and services together in one place for the first time. Use the search function to find support near you for whatever challenge you are facing.

About the Author

Dorothea Bickerton was born in Calcutta, India, in 1929. On her family's return to the UK, she was educated in Birmingham where she studied drama. A talented actress and singer, she gave up her theatrical career in 1957 when she married and devoted herself to raising a family of three boys. After briefly emigrating to Australia, she earned a degree in  English literature and drama from Sydney University, in 1970. Her daughter was born in England in 1972, after the family's return.

Dorothea's life changed dramatically when her eldest son, David, turned to drug use as a teenager in the late 1970s. As a direct result, in 1985 she founded and led one of the UK's first support groups for the relatives of drug users. For several years David worked alongside his mother as a counsellor, helping her to broaden the support available to users and their families. She received several awards for her work, before retiring as director of the charity in 2000, at the age of 70.

CDARS (Community Drug and Alcohol Recovery Services) – as the group Dorothea founded is now known – has grown to become one of the UK's leading resources for those suffering drug and alcohol addiction. Dorothea passed away peacefully in 2019, aged 89.

Printed in Great Britain
by Amazon

26504644R00076